P9-BJX-056

The Court-Martial of Lieutenant
Henry Flipper

The Court-Martial of Lieutenant Henry Flipper

By Charles M. Robinson III

The University of Texas at El Paso
Southwestern Studies No. 100
1994

Texas Western Press
The University of Texas at El Paso
El Paso TX 79968-0633

First Edition
Library of Congress Catalog Card No. 93-060328
ISBN 0-87404-196-1

Texas Western Press books are printed on acid-free paper, meeting the guidelines for permanence and durability of the Committee on Production Guidelines for Book Longevity of the Council on Library Resources.

Frontispiece: Henry O. Flipper, West Point class picture, 1877. *(United States Military Archives)*

To Jean and Robert Cruz

Contents

Acknowledgments

Many people and organizations were involved in this project, among them the United States Military Academy Library, West Point, New York; the San Benito, Texas, Public Library; Southwestern Collection, Texas Tech University, Lubbock; the United States National Archives; Arizona State Historical Society; Rupert C. Richardson Research Center, Hardin-Simmons University, Abilene, Texas; and John Joerschke, Western Publications, Stillwater, Oklahoma.

Special thanks go to Maj. Benjamin M. Yudesis, USA (ret.), for background information on military justice, and the system for courts-martial in the nineteenth century; Mary Williams, Fort Davis National Historic Site for photographs and information on the Flipper Affair; Barry C. Johnson, Birmingham, England, for permission to quote from his book, *Flipper's Dismissal*, and his overall encouragement in this project; Dale L. Walker, Texas Western Press, for his suggestions and encouragement; my wife, Perla, and many other friends and relatives.

The facts of the Flipper Affair are a matter of public record. The conclusions drawn from those facts are entirely my own.

INTRODUCTION

The Army on Trial

On 17 September 1881, a young army officer faced court-martial in the isolated frontier post of Fort Davis. That, in itself, was nothing unusual. Courts-martial were common in those days, there being few alternative forms of judgment in the army. Many an officer stood before a board on charges often far more serious than those in this case. In this trial, however, the difference was that the defendant was black. In fact, he was the only black officer in the army.

The court-martial of 2d Lt. Henry Ossian Flipper, Tenth United States Cavalry, was not simply the trial of a soldier. To some degree, the army itself was on trial. In dismissing Flipper from the service, it failed the test.

A peculiar set of circumstances combined with his own personality to make Flipper a symbol of the legal and social upheavals of his day. Growing up a slave, he received opportunities denied to many free white children of the period. As a cadet at West Point, he learned from the experiences of others and was successful. As an officer, he became arrogant, and sometimes deliberately seemed to court disaster by flaunting long-established, if unjust, codes of social behavior. In our time, Flipper might have helped break the color barriers and bring about change. But he did not live in our time. He lived in an age when the color of his skin, combined with his own incredibly poor judgment, could blot out any previous achievement. In the arbitrary world of military justice, Flipper's trial was fair; the sentence was not.

Blacks had served in various capacities outside the formal military structure since the Revolutionary War. Ironically, the concept of black soldiers first gained currency in the South, where individual Confederate States began recruiting volunteer units of free blacks even before the first Battle of Manassas.[1] One such unit, the Louisiana Colored Troops, even went so far as to have black commissioned officers.[2] On a national level, though, no such effort was made. Blacks served as laborers and transporters in Confederate government forces, not as soldiers. When the war continued with no end in sight, the army began pressing for enlistment of black regular troops. The general government resisted, its leaders arguing that a nation-wide recruitment of blacks would lead to emancipation which in turn would bring the end of the very society which the Confederacy was established to protect. By February 1865, however, military realities forced the government to advocate formation of black regiments in exchange for emancipation. It was too late; the war was nearly over and black regular units were never organized.[3]

In the North, enlistment of blacks into the United States Army was dictated by both altruism and military necessity. Concerned with maintaining the loyalty, or at least the neutrality, of slaveholding border states which had remained in the Union, Abraham Lincoln and his advisors initially took pains to establish that slavery was not an issue, and abolition not an objective of the war. For that reason, the government flatly opposed formation of black military units and even encouraged the return of fugitive slaves to their owners.[4]

Lincoln's position infuriated abolitionists, as well as prominent black leaders such as Frederick Douglass. Douglass demanded not only emancipation, but the formation of black regiments, which would allow them to fight for their freedom. The Western states, often more strongly and violently abolitionist than the East, refused to observe the government's order to return fugitive slaves. Some states offered black units to the federal government, which rejected them.[5]

As the war dragged on, however, the abolitionists gained control, and by mid-1862, emancipation was an issue. In July, Congress gave Lincoln discretionary power to enlist black soldiers.[6] The president, though, was not ready to employ them as combat troops, preferring instead to use them, as the Confederacy did, for labor. This brought mixed reaction. Some thought it beneath the dignity of the federal government to accept black help in winning the war. Others recognized the political tightrope on which Lincoln was perched, and accepted the decision. For the abolitionists, however, it wasn't good enough and papers such as the *Chicago Tribune* attacked the president for not using "every loyal arm," including black ones, to win the war.[7] Yet the decision was already being taken away from the government by some Union officers, acting on their own and without authority, who were forming black units. This development was brought by purely military considerations. As more of the South was occupied, the army found itself with a large population of newly freed slaves. Some generals considered it good policy to withdraw them from the region, fearing they might again change hands and serve the Confederacy; others argued they might be armed and turned against the South. As historian Bruce Catton noted, by the end of the first full year of fighting, Union leaders knew the war was far from over and many more federal soldiers would die. If a portion of the army consisted of black troops, the chance of losing an equivalent number of whites was diminished.[8]

One of those acting on his own was Gen. David Hunter who, in May 1862, ordered the enlistment of former slaves in occupied areas of South Carolina, Georgia and Florida. Because of government resistance the regiment was not formally mustered until January of the following year. By then, the first official federal black regiment, the Louisiana Native Guards, had been mustered in occupied New Orleans on 27 September 1862, at the instigation of Gen. Benjamin F. Butler.[9]

The Union had an even harder time instituting a black officer corps. Butler had tried to use black officers in his Native Guards, but had discontinued them because of conflicts with white officers. It was generally understood throughout the federal system that blacks would be limited to enlisted and non-commissioned ranks, while officers would be white.[10] Nevertheless, about seventy-five black commissioned officers ultimately served in the Union Army, with even more serving as line officers.[11]

Despite political and social opposition, black soldiers were an unqualified success. By July 1865, three months after the end of the war, the United States Army had 123,156 black soldiers in infantry, cavalry, light artillery, and heavy artillery. The number was diminished, however, by the rapid demobilization of the armed forces, to such an extent that the number of active military personnel reached an alarmingly low level, particularly in view of conditions on the frontiers.[12] In the West, the Indians had taken advantage of the wartime withdrawal of troops to initiate a series of devastating depredations. In Mexico, the Republicans of Pres. Benito Juárez were in a life-or-death struggle with Maximilian's Imperialists, and conditions on that border were chaotic. More troops were needed, and many who had been mustered out at war's end, before their terms were completed, were recalled to active duty. These included blacks, some of whom had signed three-year enlistments as late as 1864.[13]

On 28 July 1866, as part of the postwar reorganization of the army, Congress authorized six new black regiments, two of cavalry and four of infantry.[14] The following month, U.S. Grant, commanding general of the army, ordered the organization of the two cavalry regiments, which were numbered Nine and Ten. Command of the Tenth was given to Col. Benjamin Grierson, a former music teacher with a brilliant career as a Union cavalry officer.[15] The choice could not have been better. Grierson, tough but humane, was fiercely protective of his troops. To him, they were simply soldiers and, although the unit was official designated "Tenth Regiment of Cavalry (Colored)," he refused to allow the word "colored" in company reports.[16]

One of the problems faced by commanders of black regiments was the quality of the soldiers. The government set high standards for the officers in those units, and the officers, in turn, expected high standards of the troops. Dissatisfied with the abilities of newly emancipated slaves, they opened recruiting offices in the northern states, in order to attract blacks with a broader background. Even so, the regiments had more than their share of backward former field hands and, because of this, officers in black units had to give more attention to detail, overseeing everything from their sanitary needs to minor paperwork—jobs which in white regiments were often handled by sergeants and clerks. As one sergeant of a white cavalry regiment remarked:

> The intimate and practical knowledge of the requirements of the men thus obtained, in addition to the greater responsibility thus placed on their shoulders, accounts for the marked efficiency I have noticed among [the officers of black units] as a class.[17]

In the black regiments, close supervision by officers in charge led to a successful soldier; lack of it could cause trouble. That lack of close supervision would play a key role in Henry Flipper's downfall as an officer.

Flipper's commission as an officer was, in itself, an anomaly, since it was generally understood that commissions were the prerogative of whites. In fact, the legislation authorizing the black regiments provided that officers would be white[18] and, although army regulations were subsequently revised to allow black officers, the post-war military nevertheless was a world with clear barriers of color. Each crossed to the other side at peril. Flipper crossed that line by accepting an appointment to the United States Military Academy at West Point, New York. There, the federal government would train him for four years to become a black officer in an exclusively white domain.

Black cavalrymen on parade ground, Fort Davis, 1875.
(Fort Davis National Historic Site)

CHAPTER

ONE

The Black Cadet

Henry Ossian Flipper was born in Thomasville, Georgia, on 21 March 1856. He and his mother, Isabella Buckhalter, were the property of the Rev. Rueben H. Lucky, a Methodist minister. His father, Festus Flipper, belonged to Ephraim G. Ponder, a prosperous slave trader.[1] As a Ponder slave, Festus Flipper enjoyed a rare, but not entirely unknown situation for bonded people in the South. Many of Ponder's people were highly skilled, and their master allowed them to contract their free time. "Mr. Ponder would have absolutely nothing to do with their business other than to protect them," young Henry later recalled. "These bonded people were therefore virtually free. They acquired and accumulated wealth, lived happily, and needed but two other things to make them like other human beings, viz. absolute freedom and education."[2] Even so, the Ponder arrangement ultimately allowed Festus Flipper to purchase his wife and children (for now there was a second son, Joseph) from Lucky.

Fortune continued to favor the Flippers, who had relocated to Atlanta when Ponder married a woman there. The household was in domestic turmoil, and eventually Ponder left his wife and returned to Thomasville. Under the marriage contract, neither he nor his wife could sell anything without the other's consent, and Mrs. Ponder had little interest in the day-to-day activities of the slaves. Left to their own devices and free of any real interference, they continued to develop their business interests. One had a basic education and obtained permission to open a night school in the woodshop. Here, at the age of eight, Henry began learning to read, write, and cipher.[3]

As the Union Army approached Atlanta, Mrs. Ponder and the slaves took refuge in Macon. Then, in the spring of 1865, Festus Flipper took his wife and sons back to the ruins of Atlanta, moving into one of the few houses that remained. Flipper's personal holdings here intact and, when compared to many whites in the city, the family was well-to-do. One of their neighbors was a former Confederate captain, whose wife was hired to tutor the two boys. In March 1866, they transferred to one of the new schools opened by the American Missionary Association, and in 1869, they enrolled in the association's Atlanta University.[4]

In the fall of 1872, Henry was sitting in his father's workshop, when he overheard a conversation about the cadet then representing the Flippers' congressional district at West Point. As that cadet would graduate the following June, there would be a vacancy, and he decided to apply.[5]

Although it has been hinted that Henry Flipper owed his appointment to Reconstruction, this was not the case. Initially black advancement in the South had been assured by the various Reconstruction governments, but the situation in Georgia had changed. Reconstruction there had effectively ended in 1870, when the Democrats regained control of the state and began passing a series of laws designed to disenfranchise blacks and remove them from the political scene.[6] If Flipper hoped to enter the academy, a Republican would have to be elected from his own congressional district and even then, he would have to show he was worthy. When Republican J.C. Freeman was elected from the fifth district of Georgia, Flipper wrote to him, asking for a nomination. After obtaining endorsements from prominent local Republicans, Freeman advised him of the various entrance requirements. On 21 April 1873, Dr. Thomas Powell of Atlanta, the family physician, examined Flipper and certified him as meeting the academy's physical requirements. He was also examined for academic ability and declared proficient. Six days later, Freeman sent the nomination to the secretary of war[7] and, on 17 April 1873, Flipper filled out a form acknowledging his candidacy.[8]

Five other blacks were appointed as cadets before Flipper, but most either had been rejected or dismissed.[9] By the time he arrived on 20 May 1873, only James Webster Smith remained. Smith, the first to enter, had been introduced to discrimination upon arrival at West Point, when he had been refused a meal at the government-owned Rose Hotel.[10] Shunned and harassed at the academy, he began retaliating and soon gained a reputation as a troublemaker. Smith also took his case to a newspaper which, while it brought reprimands against some of the cadets who tormented him, alienated those on the academy staff who might have otherwise helped him.[11]

Experience had mellowed Smith to some extent by the time Flipper arrived, and he sent Flipper a letter warning him of pitfalls and how to avoid them. "It was a sad letter," Flipper remembered later. "I don't think any thing has so affected me or so influenced my conduct at West Point as its melancholy tone."[12]

Flipper's first day was likewise unpleasant. As he walked from the adjutant's office to the barracks after checking in, he was jeered by some of the cadets standing at the windows. He realized he would not only have to face the basic prejudice of the white cadets, but also the impression of blacks as a whole created by Smith. That notwithstanding, he and Smith became friends, and within a few days, were joined by another black candidate, John Washington Williams. Flipper and Williams both did well on their preliminary examinations, but on the semi-annual reexamination, six months later, Williams was found deficient. He was brought to Flipper for tutoring; despite that, he failed and was dismissed. Then, in June 1874, Smith failed one of his examinations and was also dismissed.[13]

Now alone at the Point, Flipper found that white cadets who tried to be friendly were soon told by their peers to avoid him. Unlike Smith, he did not try to intrude and generally was left alone. Only when the abuse infringed on his class privileges did he make an issue of it, and in such cases, he was upheld. Aside from his loneliness of the next three years, his memoirs of that period show his experiences to be similar to those of other cadets, and in some ways, perhaps more pleasant; as a social outcast he was spared much of the hazing and other harassments inflicted on plebes by upperclassmen. Gradually, his quiet dignity won the respect of the others.[14]

On 23 August 1876, another black cadet, Johnson Whittaker of South Carolina, arrived at West Point. It is unlikely that Flipper and Whittaker became very close, as the new cadet was three years junior, and Flipper was always mindful of his class privileges. Their relationship appears to have been friendly, but correct. Flipper's influence, however, was obvious in Whittaker's conduct. Both disliked Smith's belligerent attitude, and Whittaker followed Flipper's example of ignoring minor insults while standing his ground when his rights were infringed upon.[15]

Henry Flipper graduated on 14 June 1877. As he marched up to receive his diploma, a cheer went up from his classmates. He finished fiftieth in a class of seventy-six, with a commission as a second lieutenant in the United States Army. Within a month, he

*Col. Benjamin Grierson, Tenth Cavalry, Flipper's
regimental commander.* (National Archives)

had been appointed to Col. Benjamin Grierson's Tenth Cavalry, stationed on the Texas frontier.[16]

The Tenth was scattered in posts across the Texas plains and the Indian Territory. Flipper was ordered to join his unit, Company A, at Fort Concho, Texas, but on arrival in Houston, learned the company was en route to Fort Sill, Indian Territory. When he reached Sill, he was made post signal officer. The signal service was not the specialized branch it is today and many of the duties, such as night signaling with torches, telegraphy, and establishing and opening communications between two points, were part of the standard curriculum at West Point.[17] In addition to signaling, Flipper handled miscellaneous duties, including supervising the survey and construction of a ditch to drain a boggy area on the post, and temporarily commanding one of the other companies when all its officers were absent. He began compiling his memoirs, which were published in 1878 as *The Colored Cadet at West Point*.[18]

These memoirs, written while Flipper was young, just graduated, with his army career and life ahead of him, may be viewed as fairly reliable. A second set of memoirs, *Negro Frontiersman*, is less so. Written in 1915, *Negro Frontiersman* reads like a tainted self-justification which, to a great degree, it is. By then, it had been established beyond any doubt that, whatever his good points, Flipper had lied to his commanding officer, been negligent with government funds, brought allegations against officers no longer alive to defend themselves, and contradicted himself on many points.

All that was in the future, however. For the present, Flipper's introduction to the army in the field was pleasant. The commander of Company A, Capt. Nicholas Nolan, was a tough professional soldier from Ireland and the regiment's most experienced Indian fighter. Soon after the company's arrival at Fort Sill, Nolan, over fifty and a widower with two small children, went to San Antonio, where he married Annie Dwyer, a twenty-one-year-old Irishwoman. The new Mrs. Nolan and her sister, Mollie Dwyer, returned to Fort Sill, where the family insisted that the bachelor Flipper board with them. He and Mollie "became fast friends and used to go horseback riding together."[19]

Captain Nolan considered Flipper "all that West Point turns out."[20] He noted Flipper's relationship with the other officers in the company was cordial, and the more they came to know him, the more they considered him worthy of his position.[21]

Although Flipper at first moved carefully around the other officers, he gradually began to see himself as their social equal. In fact, as the only black officer, he seems to have enjoyed a certain celebrity status. In one instance, Flipper's company was on an extended scout and, after four months in the field, went to Fort Concho to resupply. "We camped near the Post and there was a constant stream of colored women, soldiers' wives, etc., to see the colored officer," he recalled.

During that same encampment, however, an incident occurred which reminded him that he had no special position. One day Lt. Wallace McTear of the black Twenty-Fourth Infantry came to camp to inform Flipper that the officers of Fort Concho were planning a dinner in his honor, giving him the time and date. The next day, however, McTear returned, apologized, and told Flipper that Maj. Anson Mills, commanding the post in Colonel Grierson's absence, had forbidden it, even though Mills was a member of Flipper's regiment. Since the other officers were still friendly, he appears to have written the incident off as a quirk in Mills' personality.[22] In view of his later support of Flipper's reinstatement, it is possible that the thoroughly professional Mills simply objected to a dinner honoring a junior officer for no particular reason besides color (assuming, of course, that such dinner plans actually existed and were not a product of Flipper's vivid post-army imagination).

In the spring of 1880, Flipper's company, along with two companies from Fort Sill, was transferred to Fort Davis, in the Trans-Pecos area of West Texas. The Warm Springs Apache Chief Victorio had led an outbreak, and was now terrorizing the Southwestern United States and Northern Mexico. Colonel Grierson moved his headquarters from Fort Concho to Fort Davis to organize a campaign in conjunction with his Mexican counterpart, Gen. Joaquin Terrazas. Company A was sent to Fort Quitman, on the Rio Grande, where Nolan was advised that Victorio had raided a picket post downriver, killed several soldiers, and carried off most of their equipment and horses. Flipper was sent to inform Grierson, camped at Eagle Springs, ninety-eight miles away. He made the ride in twenty-two hours, after which Grierson threw back Victorio and drove him into Mexico, where he was eventually killed by Terrazas' forces. The following year, when Flipper desperately needed a friend, Grierson wrote a recommendation, praising his character and "his efficiency and gallantry in the field."[23]

Links in a Chain

Named for then-Secretary of War Jefferson Davis, Fort Davis was established in 1854 to protect the road between San Antonio and El Paso. It was destroyed during the Civil War, so that the post Flipper knew was a reconstruction begun in 1867. There was a large parade ground, with enlisted barracks on the east side, officers' houses on the west, headquarters, quartermaster, commissary and post chapel on the north, and post trader on the south. Except for the south, where Sleeping Lion Mountain blocked expansion beyond the trader's building, the quadrangle was surrounded by support structures, such as hospital, stable, corrals, guardhouse, and quarters for servants and laundresses. The post commander had a house to himself. Other officers shared duplex quarters, divided down the center by a common hallway. The kitchens were detached structures to the rear.

As a reward for his services in the field, Flipper was named acting assistant quartermaster and acting commissary of subsistence (A.C.S.) of Fort Davis. These positions made him responsible for "the entire military reservation, houses, water and fuel supply,

General view of Fort Davis, Texas, 1886, showing the post as Flipper knew it. (Fort Davis National Historic Site)

transportation, feed, clothing and equipment for troops and the food supply."[1] He was also responsible for a great deal of money, since the Subsistence Department was legally empowered to sell goods from the post's stores to officers, enlisted men and, under certain conditions, to civilians. Flipper received payment for subsistence goods, and generally had more money on hand than was needed for the post. After closing the books each month, he was required to transfer surplus funds to the chief commissary officer of the Department of Texas in San Antonio, withholding one hundred dollars for contingencies. However, transfer was to be made only when it could be done safely, and through checks turned in by the officers. In addition, each A.C.S. was required to send a weekly statement of funds to the chief commissary in San Antonio.[2]

Flipper always claimed his downfall began with the rides with Mollie Dwyer, who had moved to Fort Davis as part of Captain Nolan's household. His later writings indicate he may have been in love with her; when she began riding with another man, he was obviously jealous.[3] The other man was Lt. Charles Nordstrom, post adjutant, who, Flipper said, "had no education and was a brute. He hated me and gradually won Miss Dwyer from her horse back rides with me and himself took her riding in a buggy he had." To aggravate the problem, Flipper and Nordstrom shared duplex quarters connected by a common hall.

There also appears to have been some other sort of alienation between Flipper and officers, for the camaraderie of previous assignments was gone. He not only disliked Nordstrom, but now felt most of the other officers were "hyenas."[4]

As 1881 dawned, another event occurred which became a link in the chain leading to Flipper's fall. On 28 December 1880, Charles Berger, a civilian scout employed by the army, applied to Nordstrom for ten days' leave and a government horse to go to Fort Stockton. As Berger was an employee of long standing and thought to be a good character, permission was granted, and Flipper was authorized to furnish a horse.[5] Berger then disappeared with the horse as well as beef vouchers from the quartermaster's department, and on 8 January 1881 was listed as a deserter. A board, convened to look into the case, determined that neither Flipper as quartermaster, nor Maj. N.B. McLaughlin, post commander, was responsible for Berger's actions or the missing property, and recommended that Flipper drop the horse from his returns.[6]

Flipper subsequently drew Berger's pay of sixty dollars for the entire month of January, reimbursed the post trader twenty dollars which Berger owed, and kept the balance as cash on hand. He reported these facts to both McLaughlin and his successor, Col. William R. Shafter. This innocuous financial arrangement would be used against Flipper later in the year.[7]

McLaughlin, an experienced soldier considered by Flipper to be "a fine officer and gentleman,"[8] was relieved by Colonel Shafter on 12 March 1881. Shafter, who also commanded the First Infantry, was a superb officer, whose operations against Indians had won him the nickname "Pecos Bill." He had commanded black troops during the Civil War, and had been second in command of the black Twenty-Fourth Infantry on the frontier. But he was known as a martinet, who played favorites, and harassed subordinates he disliked.[9] Events would also show he had racist leanings. Shafter, a field soldier, had no particular interest in the routine, day-to-day administration of the post. The burden of commissary accounting fell totally on Flipper with no reliable reexamination, forging another link in the chain to Flipper's fall.

One of Shafter's first acts on assuming command was to relieve Flipper as quartermaster, and inform him that he would also be relieved as commissary as soon as a replacement could be found. There was nothing irregular about this, since new commanders frequently filled those positions with officers from their own regiments. In fact, Shafter also replaced Nordstrom with Lt. Louis

Col. William R. Shafter, First Infantry, commanding officer of Fort Davis. (Fort Davis National Historic Site)

Wilhelmi, his own regimental adjutant. Flipper, however, would make much of it in later years, even claiming that Shafter, Nordstrom, and the Prussian-born Wilhelmi "began to persecute me and lay traps for me...never did a man walk the path of upright-ness straighter than I did, but the trap was cunningly laid...."[10]

Although Flipper said he expected to be relieved as A.C.S. in "a few days," these stretched into weeks. Then, on 2 May 1881, Maj. Michael P. Small, chief commissary of subsistence in San Antonio, notified all post commissary officers in the department that he would be absent from headquarters for the remainder of the month, and that no funds were to be remitted to him until June. Meanwhile, Shafter continued to inspect commissary funds and sign the weekly statements until 28 May. After that, there was no inspection of funds, no weekly statements were submitted, and apparently no one inquired why.[11]

Without regular submissions to San Antonio, the commissary procedures at Fort Davis became haphazard, with no serious attempt by either Flipper or Shafter to make sure everything was in order. When Small extended his absence from headquarters into the latter part of June, Flipper found his department short on funds. He was not particularly concerned, since part of it was his own "considerable bill" yet unpaid (later testimony showed he owed $1,121.77 on his own account), and part, he knew, was owed by soldiers and laundresses, and would be collected.

On 29 June, Small, now back in San Antonio, asked Flipper for all subsistence funds as of 30 June, as soon as possible after closing his books for the month and deducting post expenses.[12] The letter arrived on 8 July by way of post headquarters, where Shafter saw it and ordered Flipper to submit his funds for inspection immediate-ly. Flipper went to his quarters, where he kept the money in a trunk, and found himself still short, this time by a very substantial amount. Between two hundred and three hundred dollars were owed by officers on detached service or in the field, and since

Shafter refused to inspect until all funds were in, Flipper borrowed that amount for the occasion. To cover the balance, he included a personal check for $1,440.43. Satisfied, Shafter told him to forward the funds to San Antonio. The following day, Flipper gave Shafter his weekly statement which said, "In transit to...Dept. [of] Texas, San Antonio, Texas, $3,791.77." This was false; the available funds, still far short of the amount due, remained scattered haphazardly about his quarters.[13]

Flipper knew he could cover part of it by collecting from absent officers when they returned to post. The balance was another matter, since he did not have a bank account to cover his $1,440.43 check. He was owed what he believed to be a large royalty payment on his autobiography, and could only hope that it would reach him in time to cover the check. Major Small had again left San Antonio for an inspection tour, and Flipper knew he would be gone until the end of July. Meanwhile, he continued to submit weekly reports to Shafter, listing the money as being "in transit."[14]

On 5 August, Small telegraphed Flipper that he had not received the funds, and again requested the transfer. When he received no reply, he telegraphed Shafter, informing him that funds reported by Flipper as mailed on 9 July had not been received. After consulting with Flipper, Shafter replied:

> Lieut. Flipper tells me three thousand seven hundred and ninety one dollars and seventy seven cents all in checks was mailed to your address July ninth. Books show that account transferred. No record of letter of transmittal or of number or description of checks. Lieut. Flipper states the letter endorsing this amount gave a description of each check and the amount for which it was drawn. Please telegraph me at once if it has not come to hand.[15]

When Small confirmed that he had no such record, Shafter examined the books of the Subsistence Department, which showed $3,791.77 transferred to Small on 9 July; it was listed "in transit" until the report for the week ending 6 August, when it was dropped from the books. Flipper said he had no record of the checks or copy of the letter of transmittal, since he had handled the business in his quarters late at night, and enclosed everything in an envelope addressed to Small, which he had mailed himself.

Because Flipper had failed to keep a record of the transaction, Shafter decided to relieve him the next morning, replacing him with Lt. Frank H. Edmunds.[16] He advised Small of the change, saying:

> Lieut. Flipper says he sent the checks and invoices in one package by mail July ninth. He kept no record of checks or letter of transmittal. The checks missing are dated between April seventeenth and July ninth & he says he endorsed to you. I have stopped payment on all checks to Flipper as A.C.S. between those dates. A large part of the amount was received from officers by check. Of all such I can get full description and forward by today's mail....Lieut. Flipper has been a very good and attentive officer but his carelessness in this transaction is inexcusable.[17]

At this point, Shafter did not seem to feel that Flipper was guilty of anything besides gross negligence.[18] One thing bothered him, however – late that afternoon, in the town of Fort Davis about a mile down the road from the post, he had seen Flipper's horse with saddlebags attached. The more he thought about it, the more he worried that Flipper might be trying to desert with the missing money. The adjutant, Lieutenant Wilhelmi, was sent to bring Flipper back to the post, where he was ordered to give Lieutenant Edmunds all public funds then in his possession, "something over two thousand dollars," before leaving his quarters. Shafter was also disturbed by Flipper's "very unconcerned manner" and by the fact that Flipper had not informed him of Small's first telegram of 5 August.

The next morning, Shafter informed Flipper that Edmunds and Wilhelmi were going to search his quarters and inspect his personal checkbook. If everything were in order, Shafter assured Flipper he would apologize, but if anything were out of line, he would be arrested.

In searching Flipper's desk, Wilhelmi and Edmunds found three hundred dollars with letters of transmittal, as well as weekly statements for July, signed by Shafter but not mailed. This left a very large deficiency of funds. They seized various articles of Flipper's personal property, including his West Point class ring. After informing Flipper he was under arrest and confined to quarters, Wilhelmi went into the hallway, where Edmunds told him he had noticed some cinders in the fireplace "which might be the remains of checks." Flipper was confined to his quarters under an armed guard, who was told to hold him incommunicado and not allow anything in the room to be disturbed. Then Wilhelmi reported to Shafter, who accompanied him back to Flipper's quarters.[19]

Suspicion now turned toward Lucy Smith, Flipper's housemaid, whose belongings were found in his trunk. The officers found her cleaning when they arrived, and Shafter asked her if she knew Flipper was in trouble. She said she did not, nor did she claim to know anything about Flipper's business. Shafter ordered her back to his office, where a search yielded $2,853.56 in checks, of which $432.60 were negotiable, concealed in her clothing. Of these, $1,413.13 were checks given to Flipper by officers of the post in payment for June and July commissary bills, along with Flipper's check for $1,440.43. These were the checks which Flipper had told Shafter were endorsed to Small and mailed on 9 July. Lucy Smith was charged with theft of government property and sent to the county jail in Presidio.[20]

Shafter was now convinced that Flipper had intended to embezzle the money. To department headquarters, he wrote:

> The amount embezzled by Lieut. Flipper is thirty seven hundred and ninety one dollars and seventy-seven cents. The checks of officers and money recovered today will reduce that amount fifteen or sixteen hundred dollars, Lieut. Flipper has stolen.
> I have confined him in a cell in the post guard house, that being the only secure place in the post, until the orders of the Department Commander can be had in his case.[21]

The "cell in the post guard house" was a stone room 6 1/2 feet long by 4 1/2 feet wide. Although the door was shut, at any given time at least fifteen ordinary soldier-prisoners, confined on various charges, were housed in the corridor just outside. No visitors were allowed without Shafter's approval.[22] This indignity on an officer sent repercussions across the nation, and on 16 August, Shafter received a telegram from San Antonio stating, "The Commanding General [Brig. Gen. Christopher C. Augur, commander of the Department of Texas] directs that you arrange for his security by providing a place other than the guard house."[23] In Washington, neither Secretary of War Robert Todd Lincoln nor General of the Army W.T. Sherman had any illusions about the reason for the confinement; General Augur received a telegram saying, "Both the Secretary of War and General of the Army require that this officer must have the same treatment as though he were white."[24] In response, Shafter ordered Flipper returned to his quarters, where the back door and window were boarded up, and a hasp and lock were placed on the front door. The front window was nailed down. A sentinel on the front porch could look into the room.[25]

Meanwhile, the civilian business community of Fort Davis, which had come to respect Flipper during his tenure, rallied to his aid. A fund drive raised almost two thousand dollars toward the

*Ruins of the guardhouse where Flipper was confined,
with cells in the foreground.* (Author's Photo)

shortfall. Even Shafter gave one hundred dollars, although he insisted it was a loan and kept Flipper's watch as security.[26] By 17 August, Shafter was able to advise departmental headquarters that Flipper had turned in $3,056.38, including checks taken from Lucy Smith and money found in his room at the time of arrest.

> He has given for the balance of his responsibility two due bills of perfectly responsible merchants of this place, due in ten days, one for two hundred (200) dollars and one for four hundred and thirty five dollars and thirty nine cents ($435.39) and a check of responsible party for one hundred (100) dollars on San Antonio National Bank to be paid at same time as due bills. I consider the whole account secure. I have taken the sentinel off his room and placed Lieut. Flipper in close arrest and until otherwise directed by the Department Commander will continue him in that status.[27]

Twelve days later, Shafter reported Flipper had "made good" all the money for which he was responsible. Edmunds sent it to Small in San Antonio, asking that the negotiable checks taken from Lucy Smith be kept by the bank, since they would be needed as evidence. Shafter had filed two charges against Flipper.[28] The first, consisting of only one specification, accused him of embezzling $3,791.77 in government commissary funds entrusted to him as acting commissary of subsistence, during the period of 8 June to 13 August 1881. The second charge was conduct unbecoming an officer and a gentleman, and consisted of five specifications. The first stated that, having been ordered by Colonel Shafter to transmit subsistence funds to the chief commissary, Flipper had, on or about 10 August, 1881, assured Shafter that the order had been carried out, "well knowing the same to be false...."

The second, third, and fourth were repetitious, the only difference being the dates of the offenses. Judge Advocate Gen. D.G.

Swaim summed them up in a report to Secretary Lincoln as follows:

> Presenting for approval to his said Commanding Officer weekly statements of funds for which he [Flipper] was responsible as Acting Commissary of Subsistence, for the weeks ending July 9th, 16th and 23d, 1881, each containing the statement that said sum of money was "In transit to the Chief Commissary of Subsistence Department of Texas;" well knowing said statement to be false, in that said sum of money was not in transit as stated, but had been retained by him or applied to his own use or benefit.

The fifth specification stated that Flipper had represented to Colonel Shafter, as part of the government funds, his personal check for $1,440.43, "which check was fraudulent and intended to deceive the said commanding officer...."[29]

Each charge and specification was considered a separate offense, with verdicts returned both on the charges, and on each of the individual specifications. The second charge, "conduct unbecoming an officer and a gentleman," was perhaps the more dangerous to Flipper's military career. It was taken from the Sixty-first Article of War, a catch-all which stated, "Any officer who is convicted of conduct unbecoming an officer and a gentleman shall be dismissed from the service." The definition of such conduct was at the discretion of the court-martial board trying the case.[30] In short, it was a means by which the army could rid itself of undesirable officers.

CHAPTER

THREE

The Court-Martial Begins

Headquarters
Department of Texas

San Antonio, Texas, September 3, 1881

Special Orders

No. 108

I. A general court-martial will convene at Fort Davis, Texas, on Thursday, the 15th day of September, 1881, at 10 o'clock, a.m., or as soon thereafter as practicable, for the trial of Second Lieutenant H.O. Flipper, 10th Cavalry.

Detailed for the court:
Colonel G. Pennypacker, 16th Infantry;
Lieutenant-Colonel J.F. Wade, 10th Cavalry;
Major G.W. Schofield, 10th Cavalry;
Surgeon W.E. Waters, Medical Department;
Captain Fergus Walker, 1st Infantry;
Captain William Fletcher, 20th Infantry;
Captain W.N. Tisdale, 1st Infantry;
Captain R.G. Heiner, 1st Infantry;

Captain E.S. Ewing, 16th Infantry;
Captain L.O. Parker, 1st Infantry;
First Lieutenant W.V. Richards, Regimental Quartermaster, 16th Infantry;
Captain J.W. Clous, 24th Infantry, is appointed judge-advocate of the court.

No other officers than those named can be assembled without manifest injury to the service.

By command of
Brigadier General Augur:
G.B. Russell,
Captain, 9th Infantry, A.D.C.[1]

Of the eleven members of the court, four were officers of the First Infantry, and therefore under Shafter's command as regimental colonel. German-born Captain Clous, the judge advocate who would present the government's case, was an officer of a black regiment and had served with Shafter against Kiowas and Comanches in 1871. At the time of Flipper's court-martial, Clous was on detached duty as acting judge advocate of the Department of Texas.

Although Flipper later contended that Clous stacked the deck by selecting the members of the court, reviewing the proceedings after the trial, and recommending "the approval of his own work,"[2] this simply is not true. As Barry Johnson pointed out in his careful analysis of the Flipper Affair, the court-martial board was selected by the adjutant general of the department (Col. Thomas Vincent), who as chief administrative officer knew which officers were available. The record of testimony was reviewed at regular intervals, allowing each witness to make corrections and the defense and judge advocate to seek any necessary clarification. All arguments on points of law and procedure were also recorded and presumably read by the departmental commander, negating the need for Clous to review or recommend anything.[3]

The judge-advocate: Capt. John W. Clous, 24th Infantry.
(Fort Davis National Historic Site)

Clous' personality does enter into the situation. In nineteenth century courts-martial, the judge advocate merely presented the government's case, administered all oaths, and questioned witnesses on behalf of the government. He was not a prosecutor in the civilian sense of the word. Clous, however, tended to prosecute, an inclination which Flipper's defense counsel would encourage during the trial, in an effort to establish a definite adversarial relationship. Another factor was that in 1881, the judge advocate, as legal representative of the government, was privy to all closed sessions of the board—something which the defense was not—and a wise judge advocate could use those discussions to benefit the government's case.[4] Given these factors, together with the number of Shafter's men sitting on the court, Flipper was, to some extent, playing against a stacked deck.

United States vs. Henry Ossian Flipper began in the post chapel/school building at Fort Davis at 11:00 A.M. 17 September 1881, two days behind schedule because Clous had been delayed by weather and bad roads. Captain Parker, who had been relieved as a member of the court, was not present. With Parker out of the case, Shafter's men had been reduced by one, leaving three of the remaining ten. Since the delay had hindered Clous' preparations, the court adjourned until 19 September.[5]

When proceedings resumed, Flipper was offered a chance to object to any member. This was an opportunity to remove more of Shafter's people from the board, but he missed it by accepting the court as presented.[6] Aside from allowing members of the First Infantry to remain, this acceptance, normally an obscure part of the formalities, later would be disputed at length.

With the preliminaries out of the way, Flipper was granted time to obtain counsel and court adjourned until 10:00 A.M. 1 November.[7] He now had to find competent representation. Military officers were prohibited from charging a fee for defending other officers, but he lacked the courage to ask one for assistance.

The post chapel at Fort Davis also served as a school and community center for the garrison, and, in Flipper's case, as a courtroom. (Fort Davis National Historic Site)

Civilian attorneys wanted at least a thousand dollars to take the case. When Flipper sent a white friend to the east to raise the money, black leaders in the major cities politely declined to become involved.

Faced with this indifference from his own people and feeling helpless, Flipper "determined to fight my battle alone and unaided, as I had always done, when, like a bolt out of a clear sky, I received a letter from Captain Merritt Barber of the 16th U.S. Infantry, white, offering to come and defend me."[8] Checking the army register, he found Barber had been judge-advocate general for one of the military departments and was therefore a competent attorney. Flipper immediately wrote Barber and accepted his help. "He came, lived in my quarters with me and made a brilliant defense, better than any civilian lawyer could have done," he recalled more than thirty years later.[9]

Barber's presence also served to balance the board. Of the nine remaining members, two were from Flipper's regiment and three, including the president, were from the defense counsel's regiment, thus offsetting the three under Shafter's command.

Court reconvened as scheduled on 1 November, with an additional officer, Col. James van Voast, detailed to the board on orders from General Augur.[10] Flipper objected, saying the order which established the court-martial and appointed its members stated that "no other officer than those named could be assembled without manifest injury to the service."

Arguing there was no valid reason for adding new members, Flipper pointed out that he was offered the right to challenge the original members of the court; he had accepted them, and by doing so, had waived his right to further challenge. Now, having waived that right with the original members and being debarred from further challenges, he said, "a new element is infused into the court, which I had no reason to expect, and which I could not and did not take into consideration."[11]

Saying Flipper's challenge amounted to a challenge to the authority of the departmental commander, Clous got a recess to prepare his reply. When the court returned, he said the statement that no other officers could be assembled was a procedural phrase and irrelevant to the case. When Clous pointed out that Augur had consulted the War Department in the matter, however, Barber protested:

> The accused is not aware that the War Department is authorized to have anything to do with the composition of this court after the department commander has exercised his prerogative, and has selected the court, and it has been organized, sworn, been in deliberative sessions and has taken the interests of my client in its charge.
>
> The record shows that the accused was satisfied with the court. The department commander was satisfied with the original detail when he made it, for he says no others could be assembled "without manifest injury to the service." The accused was satisfied when he was summoned before it because he accepted the detail without challenge. Consequently the court was organized....Now some motive must have influenced a change in its composition, and the accused has a right to feel that the motive must have been adverse....One member entirely changes the composition of the court, because [Flipper] did not consider that member.

After closed deliberation, the court upheld General Augur's right to appoint additional members, but sustained Flipper's challenge to Van Voast on the grounds of dissatisfaction. Colonel Van Voast retired from the courtroom and from the trial.[12]

At this point, Clous noted he had an "additional matter to be presented to this court for trial," which he said he had only recently been given. Consequently, he asked an adjournment to continue his preparations.[13] Barber responded by asking the record to show that Flipper had been served with the relevant charges and was ready to go to trial. Court was adjourned for two days.[14]

Late the following day, Flipper was served with additional charges stemming from the Berger affair,[15] and when court reconvened on 3 November, Barber was ready to fight. Clous, though, was one step ahead, saying it would not be proper to present these charges until after the current trial was concluded. If Flipper opted "to save time and the ordeal of two separate trials," was willing to waive the right of challenge and have the court sworn again for the second set of charges, then Clous said he would have no objection to trying both sets of charges together.[16] That said, Clous prepared to arraign Flipper on the original charges.[17]

Barber interjected that he needed to consult with Flipper on the new charges and obtained a recess. When it was over, Barber demanded to know the origin of the new charges, which during the previous session of court had not even been prepared. He did not rule out combining all charges in a single trial, but stipulated that decision could be made without further information.

Clous gave a noncommittal answer, but when Barber continued to press his demand, the judge advocate finally replied:

> I will state that the charges and specifications that I have referred to in my remarks were prepared and are signed by Colonel William R. Shafter, First Infantry. That these charges have been handed me with an order to bring them before this court, and they have been approved and ordered for trial by the department commander. I presume that information will be sufficient.[18]

The arguments continued into the afternoon and were getting nowhere. Finally, Barber said Flipper was not prepared to answer on separate trials at that point. He then asked for a list of papers and property taken from Flipper's quarters at the time of his arrest, in order to determine witnesses to call for the defense. He said both he and Flipper had asked Shafter for the list and that Shafter had repeatedly assured them it would be provided. Barber said Shafter ultimately admitted that he had given the list to Clous.[19]

Clous replied that an argument in court was a waste of time. He pointed out that army regulations prescribed how witnesses were procured, and if Barber wanted any papers or witnesses, he should make proper application. Only if Clous then failed to provide them should the matter be brought up before the court. Until that time, Clous said, "There is no use of taking up the time of the court about this matter and lumbering up the record."

"We don't know what papers you have got," Barber argued.

"You can address me on the subject, and I will give you a list of all the papers I have got," Clous said. "There is no use of lumbering up the record in that way. When I fail in that respect to do the duty imposed on me by the regulations of the army, then I think, is time enough for the accused to come before this court and complain, but not now. I have not been asked heretofore. The first official information I have had is from the accused, just now, in court."[20]

Barber apologized, but said he had reason to believe Clous had documents which were material in the defense, and which would help Flipper determine witnesses to summon. But when Barber asked the court "to instruct the judge-advocate or request him" to furnish the list, Clous bristled[21] and told Colonel Pennypacker:

> Mr. President, I again say that it is not competent for this court to take any action upon that subject until I have failed to do my duty, and I consider the request as a reflection upon me in a matter upon which I have not been asked to act. On the contrary, when I came here first to try this case, I showed him every paper I had in my possession, and since that [time] I have informed his counsel outside of court that whenever he wished to ask me about any paper I would be very glad to show it to

The defense attorney: Capt. Merritt Barber, 16th Infantry.
(Fort Davis National Historic Site)

him, and I ask the court to be cleared now to settle the matter.[22]

Barber acknowledged that Clous had cooperated up to that point, and said he would henceforth confer with Clous before bringing such matters up. Pennypacker, apparently irritated with the slow progress of the proceedings, said the time had come to arraign Flipper on the original charges. At Barber's request the arraignment was postponed until the following morning.[23] Although Barber had moderated his tone toward the end of the session, the arguments throughout the day foreshadowed the carefully orchestrated rancor which would develop between him and Clous as the trial progressed.

CHAPTER

FOUR

Shafter on the Defensive

When court reconvened, Flipper said he would agree to try the original charges and those from the Berger affair in the same court-martial and waived the right of challenge. Clous apparently now had second thoughts because, after a closed session, he responded that since Flipper's statement was not in the form of a motion or a proposition, the government intended to proceed only on the original charges and specifications, trying the new charges later.

Flipper was then arraigned for embezzlement with one specification, and conduct unbecoming an officer and a gentleman with five specifications. He pleaded not guilty to each charge and specification.[1]

As prosecution exhibits, Clous submitted Flipper's accounts current for June and July and his return of provisions for August, all of which were verified by the defendant.[2] The government then called its first witness, Colonel Shafter. Under the rules, Clous would conduct the examination-in-chief of government witnesses, with Barber restricting his cross-examination to points raised by the judge advocate. If Barber wished to move into new areas, then he was free to recall the witnesses on behalf of the defense. With defense witnesses, the roles were reversed, Barber conducting the examination-in-chief and Clous cross-examining.

Under questioning by Clous, Shafter went over events until Small notified him the money had not been received in San Antonio.[3] He said when he asked Flipper why Small's earlier message on missing funds had been withheld, Flipper replied "that he thought it was only some temporary delay in the mail, that [the money] would reach San Antonio soon, and that it was not worth while to trouble me about it. I think all that I said to him then was that I preferred to be troubled about such matters and that he should have notified me." He described Flipper's explanation about how the checks and invoices had been mailed, and said at that point he had relieved Flipper as A.C.S.

Shafter went on to say that on 12 August, he had confronted Flipper about the money, including his personal check for $1,440.43, which was not on the list of checks Flipper claimed had been sent. When Flipper said he had forgotten it, Shafter testified:

> I told him that was a very large sized check to forget, that I did not believe he had ever sent the checks and that I was going to act accordingly, that if I was doing him an injustice I would apologize to him when it was over, and if I was not, I did not care anything about it.[4]

Shafter then discussed the search of Flipper's quarters, his arrest, the interview with Lucy Smith, and the recovery of over $2,800.00 in checks found in her possession. Several of these he recognized as having been presented to him as commanding officer on 8 July, the day before he ordered them sent to San Antonio. Among those was Flipper's check for $1,440.43. After exchanging telegrams with the bank, Shafter said he went to see Flipper in the guardhouse and told him he "had no personal account with the bank and consequently his check for $1,440.00 was good for nothing and that his deficiency, instead of being about $900.00, was perhaps something like $2,300.00 or $2,400.00."

According to Shafter, Flipper replied, "Yes, Colonel, I had to deceive you in the matter in some way and I took that way to do it." Shafter said he then told Flipper, "You need not incriminate yourself – I don't want you to do so unless you choose to, but I should like to know where that money has gone to, if you are willing to tell me."

"He said, 'Colonel, I don't know where it has gone to,' " Shafter continued. "I said, 'It is very strange that you should be short $2,400.00 and not know where it is, or what has become of it.' "

"Yes, that is so, but I can't account for it unless some of them have stolen it from me," Flipper supposedly replied, to which Shafter asked, "Who do you mean by 'some of them'?"

When Flipper said he did not know, Shafter asked him if he thought Lucy Smith might have any of it. "He said, 'No, sir, I do not.' "[5]

At Flipper's request, Shafter said he met with three area merchants and citizens of Fort Davis, who Flipper felt would help make up the deficit. After visiting him in the guardhouse, the three asked Shafter about Flipper's situation if the money were repaid. Shafter said he told them it would save him from prison and that as soon as the amount was repaid, "I should release him from the guard house and place him in his quarters as I would any other officer that was under arrest." Here Shafter indicated that it was repayment of the money, rather than orders from superiors, that caused Flipper's release.[6]

Under cross-examination from Barber, Shafter said he had relieved Flipper as quartermaster almost immediately after assuming command of Fort Davis, since he planned to appoint his own regimental quartermaster to the position. From then until 10

August, Flipper had continued to serve as commissary, and Shafter acknowledged he believed Flipper had performed those duties "intelligently and entirely to my satisfaction" until the cash shortage arose. He added that about 1 July, he told Flipper he planned to relieve him from commissary duties "not because I was dissatisfied with him, but it was because I thought he ought to be assisting other cavalry officers in performing their duties in the field."[7]

"Then," Barber began, "if I understand you correctly, that up to the occurance [sic] of this matter, the conduct of Lieutenant Flipper in the transaction of his official business with you was not only satisfactory but praiseworthy?"

"I say so, as far as I knew," Shafter replied.[8]

Barber then questioned Shafter about Small's absence from San Antonio, the delay in transmitting funds, and his conversation with Flipper about keeping such large amounts on hand. As Barber pressed for more details, Shafter admitted he did not know about procedures at Fort Davis prior to his assuming command, and did not even know whether records or accounts for the previous command existed, because he had not bothered to look for them. He also admitted he had received no notice of deficiencies in Flipper's transmissions prior to July and added, "Up to that day there was not reason to think but that they were all straight."[9]

Shafter said he did not know when Small's order to hold funds at Fort Davis was received, but that it came "two or three months" before the funds were ordered sent.

"After that time, did you inspect the funds regularly?" Barber asked.

"Every week when I was present, every Sunday morning—the funds on hand, not his bank account," Shafter replied.[10]

By the time the court adjourned for the day, the *San Antonio Express* noted, "The cross-examination did not elicit anything special, save to strengthening [sic] the prosecution by more positive statements."[11] Yet as the day drew to a close, Barber was beginning to find cracks in Shafter's administration of Fort Davis which, in turn, might have affected Flipper's performance as commissary.

When cross-examination resumed the following day, Barber referred to a point of Clous' examination, asking why Shafter had obtained a list of checks from officers who had made commissary payments.

"It was taken because at the time—that I believed that the checks had been mailed, and by some means they had been lost in transit to the chief commissary at San Antonio, and I wished to get a list of the checks so that I could...have payments stopped on them," Shafter said. He added that Flipper's failure to include his own $1,400.00 check was among the things which caused him to think the checks had not been sent, "and learning that there had not been any stage robbery was another, Lieutenant Flipper's manner was another...."[12]

Shafter was beginning to stumble and Barber decided to go back over his testimony on the search of Flipper's quarters and his arrest. Now Shafter could no longer remember whether he looked at the papers Lieutenant Wilhelmi brought from Flipper's quarters, or took Wilhelmi's word as to their contents.[13]

As Barber led him into the search of Flipper's person, Shafter said he had instructed Wilhelmi and Lieutenant Edmunds to see if he was concealing money. "If he had [they were ordered] to take it. Commissary funds were found on his person as I am told."

"Do you consider his watch commissary funds?" Barber inquired.

"No, sir, [I] consider it personal property."

"That is what I desire to call your attention to," Barber said, "whether your orders to these officers to search his room and his person, and take possession of his valuables, included such articles of ornament and use as were on his person."

"I told them to take possession of everything valuable about Lieutenant Flipper's quarters, and search him and see if he had any money, and in doing that, they took his watch – they obeyed my order exactly. They were expected to bring everything that was valuable about his place and person, and it was brought to my office and locked up and, except for the commissary funds that were found on his person, it is there yet and likely to stay there," Shafter snapped.

"That, Colonel, was not asked for by the question," Barber said.

"I know it was not," Shafter replied, now clearly on the defensive.

Barber said he understood the colonel's orders "included his watch, his finger rings, his shirt studs, his sleeve buttons, his shoe buckles and other articles of personal use and ornament that were found on his person at that time."

"There was nothing designated," Shafter explained. "I directed them to take possession of everything of value. I did not tell them to take his watch, mentioning it was a watch, or his shoe buckles, but told them to take possession of everything—to search and take possession of everything valuable that they found in his quarters on or his person."

"Please answer the question definitely," Barber said.

"I have answered it, sir," Shafter insisted.

"Did the scope of your orders intend to justify the taking of those articles of personal use and ornament which he had on his person at the time? Do you mean to be so understood?"

"I do mean to be so understood," Shafter said, "that I meant that they should take everything that he would not require in the guard house, as that was where I intended to place him and, as I did not want him to have his valuables there, and took them for safekeeping...."

If that was the case, Barber asked why Flipper's belongings were not returned when he was released from the guardhouse. Shafter answered that Flipper had applied for them but "I sent him back an endorsement or a message that I had just discovered one or two new steals and as soon as that money was made good he could have his things. Mr. Flipper said that if he could be permitted to go to town he would raise the money that he had obtained of the commissary sergeant and..."

"Are you using his language?" Barber interrupted.

"I am using my own," Shafter replied. "I am using Mr. Flipper's language as given to me, as reported to me by an officer that I sent over to see him."

"Ah!" Barber countered. "You don't pretend then to give it of your own knowledge—the language of Lieutenant Flipper?"

"I do not, but I will tell you what occurred. I did give Lieutenant Flipper permission to go to town. He did so and paid the money, and then the officer went over to his quarters and told him he could have his things and he declined to take them except through civil proceedings. The things are left there yet, and I determined not to turn him over the things unless he called for them."[14]

Shafter was becoming unnerved. Barber, determining to make the most of it, turned to the interrogation of Lucy Smith.

According to Shafter, he had questioned her, then told her he was evicting her from the post and that the provost sergeant would pick up her belongings and escort her outside the military reservation. She was leaving when his orderly said she was concealing papers in her dress. Shafter said he called her back and asked her if she was carrying any papers.

"She said, 'No, sir, I have not,'" Shafter testified. "She said, 'You can see I have not,' and she pulled her dress open and disclosed the inside of her dress. I said, 'Very well.' I simply looked as I sat across my desk. She was three or four feet off."

When the orderly still insisted Lucy was carrying the papers, Shafter said, he felt her dress on the side he had not seen and discovered the packages containing some of the missing checks. Shafter informed her he was going to press charges against her and that she would probably go to prison.[15] Thus far Shafter's testimony closely matched the affidavits both he and Lucy had given to the U.S. commissioner.

"Your affidavit, then, was based upon the facts which she had told you in regard to the matter?" Barber asked.

"No, sir," Shafter replied. "My affidavit was based upon the fact that I found in her possession the property of the United States and that she was not the lawful custodian of that property, and had no right to have it."[16]

Barber then made his point, which was to challenge both Shafter's affidavit to the U.S. commissioner and his statements to the court that the interview with Lucy had been handled with propriety.

"I have given the substance of the language, and very nearly – as near as I can recollect – the exact language," Shafter insisted.

"Did you not use very violent language in your intercourse with Lucy on that occasion?" Barber asked.

"I did not."

"Did you not curse her?"

"I did not."

"Did you not threaten her?"

"I did not."

"Did you not refer in your language in abusive terms to improper relations between her and Lieutenant Flipper?" Barber asked.

"I did not," Shafter insisted. "I don't think I used an oath during the whole examination, although I am liable to, but I am very positive that I did not. On the contrary, I am sure that I talked very quietly to the girl. There were two or three persons present who heard the whole conversation."[17]

Barber was hitting points where Shafter was vulnerable; the colonel's bombast, threats, and profanity were well known in the army and earned him little affection among his officers and men.[18]

Continuing this line of questioning, Barber asked, "After finding all the checks, have you stated all the action which you took toward Lucy?" Here Shafter was penned into a corner. Answering first in the affirmative, he then reconsidered and admitted he had sent for his own female servant and ordered her to take Lucy into another room and search her.

"Did you direct her to strip Lucy?"

"I directed her to make a thorough search."

"Do you swear that you did not order her to be stripped naked?"

"I did not tell her to be stripped, but I did tell the woman to examine every part of her clothing and see that there was nothing under them," Shafter replied.

"Do you know if that was done?"

"I know that the woman told me that it was done. She told me that she made her take all her clothes off."

"Where was this done?" Barber asked.

"In my own office."

"How many persons were around the office?"

"There was no person about the office whatever but the two women," Shafter said. "About the building there was probably the regimental quartermaster, sergeant major, my orderly, and perhaps others."

When Barber asked if any soldiers were watching through the windows, Shafter replied. "I don't know. I am very positive none were at the front windows and I don't believe there was any at the back."[19]

Although Shafter's affidavit to the commissioner acknowledged that he had threatened Lucy with a strip search, this was the first mention that one had actually occurred and that there may have been male spectators. For Victorian America, where physicians routinely delivered babies under a blanket to avoid viewing the mother's body, a strip search was even more traumatic than it is today. Had Lucy Smith been white, it is debatable whether Shafter could have saved his career. As it was, his morals were now in question and, after a recess for lunch, Barber struck hard.

"Did not you tell her during that interview that if she would tell all she knew about Flipper, and tell the truth about this matter, she could have a house in the garrison, or quarters in the garrison here, and have friends among the officers, and that you would go around and see her yourself once in awhile?" he asked.

"I did not tell her any part of it, nor anything that could be tortured into it," Shafter said.

"You have stated that you did not use any violence or abusive language during that interview....Did not you say to her during that interview, `Yes, God damn you, you will go to the penitentiary, and Mr. Flipper, God damn him, I have got him when I want him'?"

"No, sir, I did not say anything at all like it except to tell her that she would probably wind up in the penitentiary, or would probably go to the penitentiary for her share of the transaction; but as far as cursing her, or swearing about Lieutenant Flipper to her, I did not do it," Shafter insisted.[20]

Barber was now trying to establish that Shafter had subjected Lucy to blatant sexual harassment, a line of questioning for which he probably had no grounds whatsoever. There was nothing in either Shafter's or Lucy's depositions to indicate that anything of that nature had occurred; nor would any subsequent testimony bring out that Shafter had said anything which could be construed as an indecent threat or proposition. Apparently Barber was using the now-acknowledged strip search as a base, allowing the imaginations of the court to follow through and totally discredit Shafter's testimony. All the while, Clous sat quietly, raising no objections. But when Barber went into Shafter's seizure of Lucy's personal effects, he protested the materiality and demanded Barber stick to things brought out in the examination-in-chief. Barber replied that it was open to cross-examination because Clous had questioned Shafter about his interview with Lucy.

Clous withdrew the objection, saying he wished to give the defense every opportunity to make its case. As Barber continued to press Shafter about specific personal items, Clous said he was going too far and insisted on a ruling from the court. Barber, on the other hand, insisted on the question. After a conference in closed session, Clous's objection was sustained.[21]

Now Barber began questioning Shafter on Flipper's confinement in the guardhouse, trying to draw out that his basic needs were not met. Once again, Clous objected.

"Whom are we trying?" the judge-advocate demanded. "This witness or the accused?"[22]

Frustrated, Barber replied, "We are not endeavoring to put the witness on trial before this court, but we are endeavoring to show that the treatment which has been administered to us has been the severest punishment that has been administered to an officer of the army since its organization."[23]

Clous's objection was overruled. Barber, however, had made his point already, and the rest of his questioning was routine. Court finally adjourned for the day at 3:00 P.M.[24] It had been a hard, brutal session. Commenting on it, the *San Antonio Express* noted:

> The defense is endeavoring to show that in the treatment of Lieut. Flipper...Col. Shafter was prompted by a persecuting spirit, not warranted by custom in the army in like cases, or the facts as they expect to develop them in due time.[25]

CHAPTER

FIVE

The Court Asks: Was Flipper Persecuted?

·The sixth day opened with a forty-minute argument between Clous and Barber over the means and methods for summoning defense witnesses. When it was over, the court ruled for Barber, and Clous had such a headache he said he would be unable "to sit here any longer." Colonel Pennypacker offered to adjourn, but Clous said a recess, allowing him to rest for awhile, would suffice. Court recessed for just over an hour, after which Shafter was recalled.[1]

Barber asked Shafter if he had any opinion of how Flipper might have used the missing money. The colonel admitted that "Mr. Flipper's habits had been such that he had not used it up himself. He was not a gambler, or was not known to be, and was not a drunkard, or was not known to be, and I knew no way how he could have got away with that amount of money, and consequently it was a mystery to me then and is to a very great extent now."

Moving to the citizen fund drive, Barber asked, "Was not their action in making up this amount of money influenced by your belief in the innocence of any guilt on the part of Lieutenant Flipper conveyed to them on that occasion?"

"I don't know what influenced them to do it," Shafter replied. He added that while he personally was convinced of Flipper's guilt, and had been at the time mentioned, he might have said something to the effect that he did not know how Flipper had done it.[2]

Once again, as on the previous day, Barber started to go over Flipper's confinement in the guardhouse. Shafter acknowledged that no one could visit Flipper without his permission, but said the citizens of Fort Davis could visit as often as they wished, to discuss ways of making up the missing funds.

Saying he intended to control visits to Flipper and subjects discussed during those visits, the colonel testified, "I did think it best to permit him to be interviewed on the subject matter of his shortage, and continued it as long as it was necessary. I don't recollect of giving any permission to see him on any other subject."

When Barber asked if he specifically recalled denying anyone permission to visit Flipper, Shafter said he believed there had been "a number of persons." The only incident he specifically recalled was when "A colored man in town that has some official position asked to see him....I asked him what he wanted. He said he wanted to see him. I told him he could not do it. I don't recollect any other, although there might have been."[3]

"Do you remember of any persons bringing a note of introduction from the United States Commissioner, who requested to see Lieutenant Flipper?" Barber asked.

"I do not."

"If such occurred, would you remember it?"

"Perhaps I might and perhaps not. I don't recollect it at this time."

Barber showed him the note, which was then handed to Clous for examination. Shafter asked that the note be read to him, then stated he still did not recall the incident, but added that based on the note alone, permission would have been denied.

"Do not you remember that a man presented that note from the commissioner, asking an interview with Lieutenant Flipper, which you not only denied but sent the man out of the garrison?" Barber asked.

"I know positive that there was no man sent," Shafter replied, then hesitated. "Well, I should like to amend my answer. I recollect the whole thing now. There was a drunken nigger that had been a servant in the garrison. He came to me drunk and asked to see Flipper....I told him he could not see Flipper. It was a drunken, worthless fellow that was very much intoxicated at the time, who could have no possible reason for seeing him. I cannot give his name without some person can tell it to me. But that is a fact."[4]

Barber ignored the racial slur, which mattered little in a nineteenth-century court, and pressed Shafter on the memory lapse. Ultimately, Shafter admitted that his memory was faulty on some points, adding he only remembered important events in the day to day administration of the post.

"You don't consider that the denial of a person in the guard house the privilege of seeing his friends, or the denial of his friends of seeing him, worthy of your recollection of the administration of the post?" Barber asked.

"I think I said that I did not recollect every little incident connected with the command of my post," Shafter replied. "I do now recollect this occurrence and I did not consider it a hardship, or that it was a hardship for Lieutenant Flipper not to see this particular man, and I did not intend, as I have said before, that he should see any person unless I know about it, and it was on proper business."

On that note, court adjourned for the weekend.[5] When it resumed on Monday, the seventh day, Barber and Clous got into another argument on the procedure for witnesses. This left Clous with another headache, and once again, court adjourned for slightly over an hour to allow him to rest. Once court reconvened, Shafter was recalled and Barber once again went over Flipper's confinement, this time in his quarters.[6]

The line of questioning had long since become redundant, and a member of the court (who was not identified in the record) had grown tired of it, saying he felt

> that I have other duties to perform for the government, that I am sent here for a particular purpose, that being to try Lieutenant Flipper for certain offenses. If there is an attempt to make out here a case of persecution, and that these acts of persecution were co-existent with the offense that may have been committed, I could see it at once, because I am a believer in the theory that persecution may, in a manner, have caused the accused to have committed certain acts.

In making this statement, the member of the court was effectively inviting Flipper to prove the conspiracy and entrapment which, over the next five decades, Flipper would claim had been prepared by Shafter and others. The member was saying he would consider it a mitigating factor in any offenses Flipper might have committed, and doubtless would have encouraged the other members of the court to consider it as well. As it was, he said everything mentioned for the past two days of testimony occurred after the supposed commission of the acts charged, and he could see no bearing on Flipper's innocence or guilt.[7]

Barber replied that the charge of the Sixty-first Article of War, concerning conduct unbecoming an officer, required an examination of all circumstances of the case. He pointed out that Flipper, an officer not yet convicted of any offense, was "confined in a felon's cell" during five days of the hottest month of the year, along with more than sixteen common soldier-prisoners at any given time.

"I scarcely know how to present a reply to a member of the court, excepting to hope that no member of the court will feel that he has any other duties more important than those to defend and guard the integrity and honor of a brother officer in the army," he said.[8]

The member acknowledged Barber's point, and said that although he still doubted relevancy, he would withdraw his objection.[9] Even so, either Barber missed the chance to prove prior persecution and entrapment, which is unlikely considering his legal skill, or he could not prove that Flipper was the victim of a racist conspiracy in the first place.

The only possible reason for dwelling on Flipper's confinement would be to reveal a vicious side of Shafter's personality – a side that might have frightened Flipper into falsifying records rather than facing the colonel with the truth. Had Barber openly raised the point, however, he would have been admitting that Flipper was, in fact, guilty of the charge. And he still could not have shown that Shafter was out to "get" Flipper from the moment he assumed command of Fort Davis.

On the other hand, Barber could establish that the colonel was far from conscientious in performance of his own duties as post commander. He introduced the weekly statements for June, one prepared for Capt. Kinzie Bates' signature as acting commander in Shafter's absence, and the other three, for Shafter's signature; none had been signed. Asked to explain this, Shafter said:

> I am positive that I always signed the statements when I examined the funds, and at no other time. It is possible that it may have been entirely forgotten and the Sunday passed by without me counting them, but if I was at the post, and my name it to the weekly statement, I know

that I counted the funds rendered on that weekly statement.[10]

The catch was that an entire month had passed with no one's signature on the weekly statement meaning, by Shafter's own admission, that the funds for that month may not have been examined at all by the responsible command personnel. Barber was to hammer away at this point again and again throughout the trial.

Barber finished his cross-examination of Shafter on the ninth day, and after a brief reexamination by Clous and a few questions from the court, he was excused. During the grueling days of examination and cross-examination, Shafter was revealed as a sloppy administrator, a racist and a martinet. Yet it was also obvious that Shafter initially entered his investigation convinced of Flipper's innocence and only later came to believe that he had stolen the money. If Barber wanted to show a conspiracy to entrap Flipper, he would have to look elsewhere.

On the tenth day of the trial, the government called Major Small, the departmental chief commissary of subsistence. Most of his testimony was simply a review of the irregularities in Flipper's accounts for the period of 4 through 24 July, when Small was absent from San Antonio, and the subsequent efforts to resolve the differences between departmental headquarters and Fort Davis. In cross-examination, Barber brought out that Small had become chief commissary on 20 December of the previous year and Flipper, already acting commissary of subsistence at Fort Davis, had come under his supervision at that time. Small testified:

> To the best of my knowledge, up to the time Lieutenant Flipper got into this trouble, [the business of the commissary] was well conducted....I had no reason to be dissatisfied with the administration of the Subsistence affairs at this post up to the time Lieutenant Flipper got

into trouble in any manner, shape or form. It was well conducted as far as I am aware, the duties were well administered.[11]

Small was excused about 12:40 P.M. After a break for lunch, his chief clerk in San Antonio, George Davidson, answered a few questions concerning transmission of funds during Small's absence from San Antonio. Barber did not cross-examine.[12]

The next witness was John Withers, cashier of the San Antonio National Bank, against which Flipper had drawn the check for $1,440.43. Withers testified that Flipper had neither a personal account, nor an account as acting commissary of subsistence at the bank. Under cross-examination from Barber, however, he acknowledged that Flipper had maintained a quartermaster's account for about three months, but had closed it in March. He also stated that on 17 August, when he had notified Shafter that Flipper had no personal account per se, the bank was holding a $74.00 certificate of deposit in his name, which had been sent by his publisher.[13]

With that, court adjourned for the day. The following morning, the government planned to call one of its chief witnesses, Lt. Louis Wilhelmi, post adjutant.

CHAPTER

SIX

The Mexican Theory

Discussing the events leading to Flipper's arrest, Wilhelmi testified that on 3 July he overheard Shafter and Flipper discussing the $1,440.00 check, and recalled Shafter as saying, "Is not this check for $1,440.00 a very large amount for an officer to have?" To that, Flipper supposedly replied, "Yes, I had a lot of small checks which I did not wish to transmit, or could not, to the chief commissary of the department, and I sent them to the San Antonio National Bank for deposit. This check represents that amount."

According to Wilhelmi, the date of that discussion was "clearly fixed in my mind as the following day was the fourth and Lieutenant Flipper had issued a circular asking the Mexicans about Fort Davis..."

When Barber objected, Clous responded that Wilhelmi was simply trying to say why he remembered the specific dates.

Picking up in mid-sentence, Wilhelmi continued, "To bring their burros here for a race on ..."

This was too much for Barber, who said if Wilhelmi persisted, he would ask protection of the court. It was obvious to him that

Wilhelmi and Shafter were trying to show that Flipper had plotted to abscond to Mexico with the missing money, and he objected "to anything about Lieutenant Flipper issuing the circular for the Mexicans," contending it was not relevant.

"It is perfectly competent for him to give the conversation that he had with the accused in that connection, and I presume he is simply giving the introductory remarks," Clous responded.

"It is perfectly evident what he is trying to give," Barber retorted.

Colonel Pennypacker interrupted, saying Wilhelmi could continue his statement and Barber could object to any part of the testimony as he saw fit.[1]

"I will not take up the time of the court," Barber replied. "Let him slash it all in, if he wants to."

Wilhelmi concluded by saying that after Flipper and Shafter had finished, he and Flipper had discussed the race which was to occur on the fourth. After describing the communications with San Antonio and the discrepancies in Flipper's accounts, Wilhelmi said that shortly before retreat on 10 August, Shafter had observed Flipper's horse with saddlebags tied up in front of Sender and Seibenborn's store in town and was afraid Flipper "might leave the post, and the country." Shafter ordered him to ride over, inform Flipper he was relieved as acting commissary of subsistence, and bring him back to the post. Wilhelmi was also told to notify Lieutenant Edmunds that he was to obtain the commissary funds from Flipper and give him a receipt.[2]

Wilhelmi carried out his instructions and, upon their return to the post, Edmunds went to Flipper's quarters to arrange the transfer of funds. Moving on to the search of Flipper's quarters, Wilhelmi testified:

> In the wardrobe in the back room, clothing of Lieut. Flipper and his servant was all mixed up. Her skirt was hanging over a pair of pants, or a pair of pants under a

skirt and a coat over a skirt – there were three pieces of clothing on the same hook. Hair brushes and combs were on the wash stand which were claimed by the servant of Lieutenant Flipper. An old tooth brush and an old comb was there, and also some bedding on the bed which she claimed belonged to her. A sewing machine was back there. It was near the bed in the main quarters.[3]

In searching Flipper himself, Wilhelmi said he and Edmunds asked him to turn out his pockets.

The first pocket that we examined was the pocket on the right hand side of his blouse. He pulled out a handkerchief and at the same time a check flew out which had been on the top of the handkerchief – of $56.00....It was a check which I had given him on the tenth of August. It was a personal check for my commissary bill for July, that of the band and the post bakery.[4]

Barber began cross-examining Wilhelmi by bringing up the circular to the Mexicans, asking them to bring burros to the post, so that officers and soldiers could race them for prizes. It developed that the race had been organized by two other officers, who had asked Flipper to prepare notices in Spanish since he spoke the language, and that Wilhelmi himself had been among the many officers who contributed prize money.[5]

Reviewing Shafter's orders to bring Flipper in from town, Barber asked if the colonel specifically expressed fears that he might leave the country.

"I think it was after the arrest of Lieutenant Flipper that Colonel Shafter said it would have been an easy matter of Lieutenant Flipper to have gone to Mexico," Wilhelmi said.

"When you returned from bringing Mr. Flipper back did you say anything to Colonel Shafter about the idea of Mr. Flipper escaping to Mexico?" Barber asked Wilhelmi.

"I think not."

"Before starting to go for Mr. Flipper did you or not, and since your report to Colonel Shafter after your return, have you not talked with him on that subject?"

"I had no conversation on that subject before starting to bring Lieutenant Flipper into this post on the evening of the tenth of August, nor when I made my report to Colonel Shafter on that evening," Wilhelmi said, adding, "At the time that Colonel Shafter said that it would have been an easy matter for Lieutenant Flipper to have gone to Mexico, I said that I believed that that was his intention on the night of the tenth, had the money not been taken from him [by Lieutenant Edmunds]. That conversation occurred after the thirteenth of August and after Lieutenant Flipper was placed in arrest."

"Then you are the originator of that Mexican theory, are you not?"

"Not at all," Wilhelmi protested.[6]

Based on the testimony so far, Shafter appears to have had an unreasonable, although very real, fear that Flipper did plan to leave the country. In bringing up this so-called "Mexican theory," however, Barber may have been trying to establish that Flipper had been framed by Wilhelmi and others, and that Wilhelmi himself was the real culprit behind the missing funds. Flipper himself harbored that suspicion, and as he grew older he became obsessed with it, even though there was never any evidence that Wilhelmi or any other officer was involved in the loss of the money.[7]

The "Mexican theory" finished for the time being, Barber guided the witness through the search of Flipper's quarters. During that search, Shafter had come in and handed Wilhelmi two envelopes with missing checks he had just taken from Lucy Smith. In all, there were thirty-two checks, including Flipper's for $1,440.43, none of which had apparently been endorsed to the chief commissary of subsistence.[8]

Wilhelmi went on to say that Shafter had returned with the officer of the day and removed Flipper, after which Wilhelmi and Captain Bates inventoried the checks. When the inventory was completed, Lucy Smith came in and removed her clothing and other personal articles from the quarters. The jewelry and money found in her trunk had been kept separate from Flipper's and was returned to her, the officers being careful to obtain a receipt for them. She was not allowed to claim bedding or the sewing machine until she could prove ownership. The search completed, the windows of Flipper's quarters were nailed down, the doors were locked and nailed, and an extra padlock was placed on the front door of Flipper's side of the building. The papers and Flipper's personal effects were placed in the safe in Shafter's office.[9]

The remainder of the day's testimony was taken up with discussions of personal property removed during the search. The following morning, at Barber's request, Shafter and Wilhelmi were present with the personal property and its inventory.[10] When Clous specifically asked what the defense hoped to accomplish, Barber replied that he wanted to see whether the list corresponded to the property. He pointed out that Flipper was never given an inventory, thus could only guess at what had been taken by going through his quarters and trying to remember what he owned. "He wants to know where it is and what it is."[11]

Clous objected to the whole line as irrelevant and immaterial to the case. To that, Barber responded, "The property is here in court, and the witness is here in court. It would not take three minutes to verify this property with the list, and then proceed with the witness, and if there are any articles about which he has testified that are missing, we can show where they are."[12]

Turning to Colonel Pennypacker and the court, Clous reviewed the charges against Flipper, then asked:

What possible bearing...will this subject of identification of the property have to enlighten you and to aid you in determining the guilt or innocence of this accused upon the subjects that I have already mentioned – the different specifications and charges? Why should you, the gentlemen of the court, sit here and permit this accused in court to verify this list? Why can't he step up like a man to his commanding officer and ask for his property? ...Was he not offered the property twice? No inventory would have been necessary, had he taken the property at the time when it was offered to him. This court would never have been troubled with the subject.

Clous added that in a civil proceeding, "The subject would be kicked out of court," and went on to question Barber's motive for bringing it up.[13]

Barber replied that he had no ulterior motive.

Everything connected with this case is proper to come before this court. What is the penalty for embezzlement? Fine and imprisonment. How much fine has he already paid? Where is the property?...We could have been half way through with the testimony by this time. It looks to me as if the judge-advocate is laboring under a terrible state of mind, that something terrible is going to take place at some other time.[14]

After more argument, the court overruled Clous and allowed the examination. Once the property was examined and verified, court was closed. When it reconvened in open session, Clous announced he had been directed to return the property to the custody of Wilhelmi and Shafter.[15] Cross-examination continued, with Wilhelmi testifying that others besides himself, Edmunds, and Flipper were present during the initial search, adding:

I don't know who it was. [I] know it was a Mexican and I told him to get out of there...they came in while we were there. There were one or two others in the back room. While we examined the back room the Mexican came into the front room, but he was in my sight all the time, and he did not take anything while we were there or touch anything. I took particular care to observe him in that respect.

Asked if the Mexican and Flipper had spoken to each other, Wilhelmi replied, "I think there was something said – just a few words....It was in Mexican [sic] and I did not understand it. I can't tell what it was."[16]

As Wilhelmi continued, it became obvious that during the search, several persons were milling about the back room of Flipper's quarters. Neither Wilhelmi nor Edmunds appears to have made any effort to note who they were, what they were doing, or otherwise control them, but allowed them to come and go as they pleased. In fact, Wilhelmi was not even certain whether they were Mexican or black, or whether Lucy Smith was among them. He indicated Flipper had divided his time between talking with the visitors and assisting in the search.[17]

Now Barber turned to Wilhelmi's brief career at West Point, in an apparent effort to show he resented Flipper's success at the academy, compared to his own failure to graduate. Wilhelmi testified he first saw Flipper at West Point in June 1873. This drew an immediate objection from Clous on grounds of relevancy and materiality.

Barber replied that he had the right to ask Wilhelmi anything about his personal life or his relations with Flipper, and the objection was overruled. Wilhelmi said originally he had been in the class ahead of Flipper, but was turned back to Flipper's class and remained in that class from 1 June 1873, until his health forced him to resign from the academy in December of that year. During that period, he did not know Flipper personally nor did he have the opportunity to speak with him.

"How long were you at the Point while Mr. Flipper was there?" Barber asked. Clous objected again, and continued to object as Barber withdrew or rephrased questions. When Clous objected to Barber's asking what Wilhelmi did after he resigned, Barber insisted on the question and was upheld. Wilhelmi replied that he went to Philadelphia and, after regaining his health, went into the insurance business which he practiced until he entered the army on 15 October 1875.[18]

"After you left the Point and up to the time that you were appointed to the army, were you at any time engaged in any detective business?" Barber then asked.

Wilhelmi replied that he was not, nor had he ever been involved in any "business of a detective character."

"This matter was your first experience?"

"Which matter?" Wilhelmi asked.

"This matter with Lieutenant Flipper."

Clous objected, and Barber withdrew the question with the comment, "I hope the judge advocate will not scold me any more than he can help and not take up the time of the court."

"I am not scolding," Clous groused. "I am simply attending to my duty, and I am responsible to no one here for it, least of all, the gentleman who represents the defense."

Winding up the cross-examination, Barber ascertained Wilhelmi's first encounter with Flipper after leaving West Point was in March 1881, when Wilhelmi was transferred with Shafter's staff to Fort Davis. Wilhelmi described his subsequent relations with Flipper as "friendly." Asked to define "friendly," he explained that while he and Flipper never visited each other socially, their working relationship was more cordial than the perfunctory formality required of officers in an official capacity.[19]

With that, Barber announced that his cross-examination was finished.

Under reexamination by Clous, Wilhelmi recalled a conversation with Flipper in the guardhouse after his arrest, in which they had discussed the falsified reports. According to Wilhelmi, Flipper explained why he had lied to Shafter by saying, "Well, you know how the colonel is, an erratic sort of man, and when he ordered me on the eighth of July to send the money off, I reported it so on the ninth."[20]

CHAPTER

SEVEN

The Government Rests

Finished, for the most part, with Wilhelmi, Clous called Lieutenant Edmunds, who testified that when he went to relieve Flipper of his commissary duties, he found a large amount of money "piled indiscriminately on his desk, currency and silver...[in] no regular order."[1] During the subsequent search which led to Flipper's arrest, he said he and Wilhelmi found "considerable money in the desk scattered around in different places, a great many private papers were in the desk, letters and other papers."[2]

After finding cash scattered haphazardly elsewhere throughout the quarters, Edmunds said he had told Flipper, "Good gracious, you don't keep all this money in your quarters, do you?" Flipper replied he did.[3]

Clous continued to elicit testimony which simply backed what Shafter and Wilhelmi had already said. Then, in a shift of tack, he introduced into evidence a letter from Flipper to Wilhelmi in the latter's capacity as adjutant, dated 17 August, asking for the return of Mexican currency and personal effects which had been taken during the various searches of his quarters.

In that letter, Flipper said the Mexican money "has been in my possession for a long time as curiosities and it is my wish to preserve them." He indicated he expected return of his personal property once the deficit had been covered, and defined the property as "my jewelry of every sort & description. I do not refer to papers of any kind." This was the application previously mentioned in Colonel Shafter's testimony, and which the colonel had endorsed.[4]

Given Clous's continual prior insistence that Flipper's property would be returned to him on application, that the application had, in fact, been made three months previously, and that the property was still in the possession of Shafter and Wilhelmi, it is incredible that Barber let the matter pass. In his book, *Flipper's Dismissal*, Barry C. Johnson reminded that Barber and Flipper had already allowed the property to be brought into court, examined, and then returned to Shafter without a word of protest. As Johnson says, "The suspicion is difficult to avoid that it suited the Defense to leave this property at post headquarters, as a `grudge' against Shafter and Wilhelmi."[5]

In short, both sides were playing games.

The letter was a prelude to Clous' introduction of Flipper's weekly statements for May, which he said were examples of testimony drawn out during cross-examination by defense.[6]

Barber replied that his cross-examination did not bring out these statements, but that Clous himself had done it in his examinations of Shafter, Wilhelmi, and Edmunds. Barber detailed the charges and specifications against Flipper, pointing out that while they were based on allegations of misconduct in July and August, Clous was reaching back into statements from a prior month. "They have no right to come before the court as illustrative of testimony – they illustrate nothing," he concluded.

Addressing Colonel Pennypacker and the court, Clous said, "Mr. President, it is very refreshing, very amusing to me that the counsel for the defense has at last sought refuge in the charges and specifications before this court. For a week or more past, he has not looked at them, I don't think, when he entered the cross-examination of this case." The papers, he said, were to lead into testimony as to Flipper's intentions, something he felt the government had every right to do.[7]

"Why don't you bring his horse into court?" Barber asked. "It might with just as much propriety come in here, according to the testimony of Lieutenant Wilhelmi."

The court was unimpressed with that bit of sarcasm, and after deliberation in closed session, overruled Barber's objection.[8]

Clous's real point for bringing up the statements came out during reexamination. He intended to prove that the deficiency dated back as far as May, and that in order to conceal that deficiency, some weekly statements for May had been erased. These statements, he said, were not forwarded, nor were statements for June or July.

> I shall attempt to show you that there was a studied attempt on the part of the accused to deceive his commanding officer from May on to July as to the real amount of funds he was responsible for.[9]

Now the government's strategy was out in the open, and Barber could only reiterate his objection that there was nothing in the charges and specifications concerning funds in May. Once again, he was overruled.[10]

Clous showed the statements to Edmunds and asked if they were in the same condition as they had been found in Flipper's quarters. The witness replied they were not, indicating the original entries had been made in ink and saying these had been erased. After recovering the statements, Edmunds explained he had checked them against the cash books in the commissary office, and noted the differences in pencil next to the erasures. Some additional notations had been made in pencil, apparently by Colonel Shafter.[11]

Barber entered another objection and Clous seized the opportunity to speculate on the defense's own line of questioning. "Since my attention has been drawn to the statements for June," Clous began, "I will make one further remark. Is it not plausible to presume...that these weekly statements for June were never presented to any commanding officer, that having made so many erasures in May that the matter could not be continued all the time without attracting attention?"

If that were the case, Clous asked, wasn't it possible that Flipper made two sets of statements, one with erasures to cover his mistakes, and one clean? The clean copies would have been presented for Shafter's signature. The erased copies, without Shafter's signature, were presented in court in an effort to show the colonel had never checked the statements for June, and was therefore himself negligent.[12] Yet, without evidence that two separate statements were made, Clous could do nothing more than speculate, and the court did not appear interested.

Barber's cross-examination was similar to his questioning of Wilhelmi. He determined that Edmunds had been Flipper's French instructor at West Point from about September 1873 until February 1875, but they had not met again until May 1881 at Fort Davis. Until the time of Flipper's arrest, Edmunds said he considered his character to be "above reproach."[13]

Bringing up the "Mexican theory" again, Barber asked Edmunds if, on the night he relieved Flipper, he had noticed anything about the latter's dress, appearance or manners, or anything in his quarters that might be suspicious.

"No, sir," Edmunds replied, "I can't say there was. Simply the large amount of money that was there. That attracted my attention and that was the only thing that did."[14]

Discussing the search, Edmunds said he told Flipper that all his personal effects would be returned to him except his watch, which Colonel Shafter was keeping to secure a loan. Shafter soon offered to return the watch as well, saying he did not want Flipper to feel pressed to repay the money. Flipper, however, declined to accept any property before consulting his attorney or except through civil authorities.[15]

After Edmunds, Captain Bates testified that he had signed Flipper's weekly statements anytime Shafter was absent.[16] That being the only question for Bates, Commissary Sgt. Carl Ross was called. He identified various statements he had prepared, but noticed erasures on several of them. He also produced a copy book showing the original amounts.[17] The questioning of Sergeant Ross was completed on 25 November, and the bulk of it simply restated everything the court had heard before.[18] The following day, after Ross had a chance to hear his testimony read back, the government rested its case.[19]

Ruins of post chapel, Fort Davis, with a plaque discussing the Flipper Affair in the foreground, portrait of Flipper visible on the plaque. (Author's Photo)

CHAPTER
EIGHT

Lucy Smith Testifies

The Flipper Affair now shared the limelight in the newspapers, since a far more important trial was under way elsewhere. In Washington, Charles Guiteau was being tried for the murder of Pres. James A. Garfield, and the scene in that courtroom made far more interesting reading than the mundane recitation of financial affairs at Fort Davis. Regarding the latter, the *San Antonio Express* reported:

> The defense in the Flipper case commenced offering their testimony...and seven witnesses were rapidly examined, and at this date it will soon bring the trial to a close.

Indeed, even Barber was surprised at how quickly the trial was now moving.[1] When Clous bothered to cross-examine at all, his questions were perfunctory.

Lt. S.L. Woodward answered a few questions on the transfer of funds from Fort Quitman, which was supplied as a subpost of Fort Davis. Captain Bates, now called as a defense witness, said that he and Capt. C.D. Vielé had organized the burro race covered in Wilhelmi's testimony and that Flipper had been asked to assist. When his turn came, Vielé could not remember any details concerning the organization of the race, only that Flipper assisted him in forming the starting line, "because I could not make those Mexicans understand me." He also testified that he had noticed Flipper's horse saddled, with bags attached, "a day or two before the arrest."[2]

The saddlebags, which Shafter had taken as an indication Flipper might flee into Mexico, were covered at length by the next witness, Walter David Cox, who had been Flipper's orderly and tended his horse since the previous 1 February. Cox said Flipper customarily carried the bags attached to his saddle, and that during the entire period since February, removed them only once, when they were repaired by the company saddler. He also testified that the bags were empty when he saddled Flipper's horse and took it to him on the day Shafter ordered him back on post.[3]

Fort Davis merchants J.B. Shields and A.W. Keesey, both of whom had loaned money to cover Flipper's deficit, testified as character witnesses. Shields, who contributed $50.00, said he knew "plenty of other citizens who would have contributed, but it happened at a very dull time, when very few except the storekeepers had any money to contribute." Asked his reasons for helping Flipper, Shields said:

> The first was because I believed he was innocent of what he was charged with. The next was I thought he was rather crowded and that it was a pretty hard place for an officer or any other man to be in a cell closed up, and from his intelligence and good behavior, I liked the man and tried to help him if I could.[4]

Under cross-examination by Clous, Shields acknowledged that during a food shortage the previous spring, Flipper had provided him with food for his family, but he understood it was from Flipper's personal mess rather than the commissary stores.[5]

Keesey testified he had provided $200.00 for Flipper's deficit, although it left him short of needed cash. He also said that he had advanced goods to the post commissary, not only under Flipper, but under every commissary officer at Fort Davis for the previous eighteen months to two years. He was reimbursed goods when the commissary was resupplied by the army although, he was quick to point out, he never quite broke even. Keesey added he met frequently with Flipper and vouched for his integrity as a man who did not gamble or indulge in "habits of disipation [sic]."[6]

Court adjourned until 11:00 A.M. 29 November[7] when, after covering procedural matters from the previous day, Barber called the witness who undoubtedly excited the most curiosity: Lucy Smith.

Lucy may have been married (during the trial, she was often referred to as Mrs. Smith); even so, it was obvious to all that she was Flipper's mistress as well as his housekeeper. In Victorian fashion, the relationship had been skirted throughout the proceedings, although at one point Clous pointedly credited himself with an effort to avoid "bringing any scandal in this case."[8] The implications, however, were too much to the contrary. During his initial testimony, Shafter referred to her as "Lucy Flipper," although he immediately amended it to "Smith."[9] Even Barber, during his examination, referred to the time that she had "lived" with Flipper, and she made no effort to correct him.[10] Free on personal recognizance pending her own trial in federal district court, and with Flipper's court-martial under way, Lucy acknowledged that she still cooked, washed, and ironed for him.[11]

Except for a trip to Fort Stockton in the spring, Lucy testified that prior to Flipper's arrest she had roomed with a Mrs. Olsup, presumably in town. While living with Mrs. Olsup, she kept her personal belongings in a trunk in a tent, which she indicated was pitched outside Flipper's quarters. She also kept some of her belongings in a trunk in Flipper's front room and in a chest in the hallway, "because I had no room, I had no place to put my things for safety and I asked him if I could not keep them in his trunk." Flipper kept the trunk locked and when she wanted the keys, she had to ask for them.[12]

So far so good. Now, however, Lucy went into memory lapses and began suffering from a severe case of fright. The farther into the questioning, the more frequent—and more convenient from Lucy's perspective—these two phenomena became. To begin with, she could not remember what happened the morning of Flipper's arrest. Under continued questioning from Barber, she did recall that she was doing the laundry and had asked for the keys to the trunk so that she could put his clothing away and get some of hers.

"Did you take out any papers and envelopes?" Barber asked.

"I taken [sic] out two envelopes....I put them in my bosom."

"What was the cause of your taking out the envelopes?"

"Because I was in this trunk and I had taken some things out, and because I had a woman in there working that was not very honest," she replied.[13]

Why Lucy could not have simply locked the trunk with the envelopes still inside was not explored by either side. It does, however, raise the question of who really might have been the dishonest woman in Flipper's quarters that morning.

Asked if Flipper had given her any instructions with the keys, Lucy replied, "He said, 'Lucy, don't go away and leave that trunk open, be very careful and keep it locked when you go away and when you go away give me back the keys.' That is what he always told me...in going away when I had the trunk open, to be sure to lock it up and hand him the keys and when I went out, to lock the doors." She said Flipper never discussed the reason, and did not mention to her anything about the papers on that particular morning.

"Then, if I understand you," Barber said, "you took them out without his knowledge?"

Answering affirmatively, she then said when she put the clothes away, she laid the keys on the table, since she had not finished with his laundry. She could not remember whether she had locked the trunk.

Although, after the initial memory lapse, Lucy seemed to have remarkable recall, the lapses now became very pronounced, together with an exceptional case of fright. She told Barber that she did not remember where she had gone after she had taken the envelopes. "I was cleaning up," she said. "I was around the house."

"You remember Colonel Shafter coming there?"

"I don't remember anything about it."

"Did you see Colonel Shafter that morning?" Barber pressed.

"I don't remember whether I seen him or not. I was so scared."

"Do you remember Colonel Shafter coming there to the kitchen and speaking to you—did you go over to Colonel Shafter's office?"

"I don't remember whether I went over there or not. I was scared to death," Lucy insisted.

"Where did you go during that day?"

"I went to jail for one place," she said.

"Where were you when you were taken to the jail? Where did you go from?" Barber asked.

"I don't know, Captain, because I was so scared, I don't know where I was taken from."

"What scared you?"

"I can't tell you that," Lucy said. "I don't know what scared me. I was scared through."[14]

Perhaps to give Lucy some breathing space – or perhaps to try the extent of her sporadic amnesia – Barber asked an irrelevant question about a ring Flipper had given her. When she had answered that in detail, he asked if she remembered what had happened to the envelopes she had taken from Flipper's trunk. Once again, she remembered absolutely nothing.[15]

One can imagine that Lucy would have been frightened on the day of Flipper's – and her own – arrest. She was a black woman in trouble with the white man's law. It is more than likely, also, that she knew a great deal about the missing money, which would have aggravated her fears. Either way, it would have certainly been traumatic for her.

On the other hand, Shafter had also suffered from convenient attacks of amnesia any time something came up which might make him look culpable. Lucy had a much better chance of doing the same and getting away with it; given the racial stereotypes of the time, the sight of a frightened black woman, wringing her hands and wailing in fear and confusion, would have raised no suspicions among the white officers of the court or the two white attorneys. Lucy's testimony, in full, shows a definite craftiness. She had contradictory memory lapses covering an entire period of several days. It is impossible to believe that of all the things that happened – her search by Shafter, her arrest, her incarceration, her statement before U.S. Commissioner Hartnett, the filing of federal charges against her – that she would not remember at least something. In short, one must conclude that she was lying all the way through.

Under cross-examination from Clous, she no longer remembered even being arrested, saying instead, "I kind of remember I was in the jail." Nor did she recall being examined by Commissioner Hartnett.[16]

"When you saw Colonel Shafter, did not he ask you whether you had any papers about you, and did not you answer him [that] you did not have anything about you?" Clous asked.

"I don't remember anything about it for I was frightened to death. That is the way of it," Lucy answered.

"You don't remember having said so on that occasion and locality?"

"No, sir. I don't remember anything about it, because I ain't got over my scare yet."[17]

In question after question, she repeated that she was too frightened to remember. She did not remember anything about the hearing before Hartnett. She did not remember telling a soldier that nothing could happen to Flipper because she "had it fixed all right." She did not recognize the envelopes which were taken from her. As for anything she might have said to Shafter, "*If I said it, I ain't responsible for it because I was frightened to death* [italics added]....The very sights of Colonel Shafter frightened me....The sights of Colonel Shafter scares me near to death."[18]

One must wonder how much of this was valid, and how much was carefully calculated by Lucy to make the colonel look bad. Subsequent testimony would show that after his arrest, when he had nothing more to lose, Flipper himself *was no longer afraid of Shafter*. In fact, he looked to Shafter to help him.

At one point during cross-examination, Clous asked Lucy if she had dressed herself in Flipper's quarters, and she answered no. Picking up on that in reexamination, Barber asked if she slept or had ever spent the night in Flipper's quarters.

"No, sir," she replied. "I went to a dance once and after I came home Mrs. Olsup and I went into the kitchen and staid [sic] there all night because we danced to three o'clock. Mr. Flipper did not know I was on the place."

"That was the only time you was [sic] there....And Mrs. Olsup was with you?"

"Yes, sir."[19]

In the end, neither Barber nor Clous gained anything substantial from Lucy Smith. If Flipper had depended on her for help or if Clous had hoped to use her against him, they were both sorely mistaken.

When Lucy was finished, one more witness, Joseph Sender, took the stand before adjournment for the day. It was Sender's mercantile establishment Flipper was visiting when Wilhelmi went to bring him back to the post. Sender's appearance as a character witness is significant to posterity primarily because of an incident illustrating the attitudes of the period: before administering the oath, Clous asked if Sender, as an "Israelite," considered it binding. Upon answering affirmatively, Sender was sworn in and testified that his firm had contributed $500.00 to cover the deficit, which amount was charged to Flipper on the company books.[20]

CHAPTER

NINE

Testimonials to a Good Name

"Fun For Flipper" was the Express's headline as a parade of witnesses marched through to testify to the defendant's good character.[1]

Barber called W.S. Chamberlain, a watchmaker at Fort Davis, who was boarding with Flipper at the time of his arrest. It was Chamberlain who had gone to the other merchants and citizens of the town and raised the money to cover Flipper's deficit. He was probably closer to Flipper than any other witness except Lucy, and now Barber hoped he would fill in some of the blanks in testimony up to that point.

Chamberlain testified that he had heard Flipper caution Lucy about the security of his room and papers "very frequently." He added he remembered that after breakfast on the morning of Flipper's arrest, they were in the front room when Lucy asked him for something. Flipper withdrew the article from his pocket and gave it to her, although Chamberlain could not be certain whether it was the key to his trunk.[2]

Shortly afterwards, Chamberlain went to his shop, where he later learned Flipper had been arrested. Because he understood Flipper was being held incommunicado, Chamberlain did not see him again until he visited him in the guardhouse the following Monday. After discussing the case with Flipper, Chamberlain went to headquarters to see if reimbursement of the money might help. He remembered Shafter as saying, "Yes, it will save him from the penitentiary....I will buck up a hundred dollars myself."[3]

Chamberlain testified that within a couple of days, he and Sender had covered the amount in cash and due bills, thus satisfying Shafter. During that conversation, the colonel told them "he always thought Lieutenant Flipper to be an honest man, and did not believe that he was guilty, that there was some one else to the bottom of it....I think his remark was that there was some `damned nigger' at the bottom of it."[4]

Chamberlain added he considered Flipper reasonably frugal, allowing himself "a dollar or two dollars" each week to attend Mexican *bailes*, but generally living within his means.[5]

The penultimate witness for the defense was Fort Davis attorney J.M. Dean, who had represented Lucy Smith during her hearing before Commissioner Hartnett. After Lucy's hearing, Dean said he overheard Shafter remark "he would get Flipper or he was on his trail, or made some remark of that sort, that he was getting more evidence on him."

"Did he say anything about piling it up on him?" Barber asked.

"Yes, sir, he said he was piling it up on him....I had been led to believe that Colonel Shafter was acting as the friend of Lieutenant Flipper and was disposed to act square towards him, but after I heard him make that remark I came to the conclusion that he was playing him double."[6]

Actually, there was no intentional duplicity in Shafter's attitude. It was simply part of the colonel's suspicious and unforgiving nature. He had trusted Flipper and believed him innocent. Flipper had lied to him about the transmission of funds to San Antonio. After finding he had been deceived, Shafter believed Flipper capable of anything, and let his imagination run wild. Then, having convinced himself that Flipper was a villain of the deepest dye, Shafter set about to prove it.

Meanwhile, Dean testified that Flipper still had confidence in Shafter, and felt the colonel was working toward clearing him of suspicion. Visiting Flipper to get information for Lucy's habeas corpus petition, Dean said:

> He led me to believe that he thought Colonel Shafter was his friend, and I told him that...from what I had heard Colonel Shafter say, that I thought it would be to his interest to conduct this matter without Colonel Shafter's assistance...that I had never heard Colonel Shafter say anything in Flipper's behalf, but on the other hand had been against him.[7]

After Dean, Maj. N.B. McLaughlin testified to Flipper's upstanding character and performance as a soldier.[8] Barber had no more witnesses, but asked to enter a letter from Colonel Grierson, Flipper's regimental commander. Although Grierson was sympathetic to Flipper, he preferred not to appear as a witness and instead had written the letter, which he desired "to be appended to the proceedings and commend him [Flipper] to the leniency of the Court and the reviewing authority."[9] Clous objected, saying that he understood if Grierson were present, he would testify to Flipper's character. However, the judge-advocate did not consider any portion of the letter pertaining to the case as being proper evidence.[10]

The letter, which was then read for the court's consideration, stated that until his arrest, Flipper's

> veracity and integrity, have never been questioned and his character and standing, as an officer and a gentleman,

have certainly been beyond reproach. He came under my immediate command in 1880, during the Campaign against Victorio's band of hostile Indians, and from personal observation, I can testify to his efficiency and gallantry in the field.

General Davidson [John W. Davidson, Flipper's commanding officer at Fort Sill], Captain Nolan and others under whom he has served, have spoken of him to me in the highest terms, and he has repeatedly been selected for special and important duties, and discharged them faithfully and in a highly satisfactory manner. Being, as an officer, the only representative of his race in the Army, he has, under circumstances and surroundings the most unfavorable and discouraging, steadily won his way by sterling worth and ability, by manly and soldierly bearing, to the confidence, respect and esteem of all with whom he has served or come in contact. As to Lieutenant Flipper's late trouble, or alleged offence [sic] for which he is now being Court-martialed [sic], I have no personal knowledge, but from all information I have been able to gain relative thereto – although he may have been careless and indiscreet, and may have committed irregularities, from want of experience, – my confidence in his honesty of purpose has not been shaken, and my faith in his final vindication is still as strong as ever...I, as his Colonel, – believing in his great promise for future usefulness; knowing that his restoration to duty would give great satisfaction to the regiment – most heartily and earnestly commend him to the leniency of the Court and reviewing authorities.[11]

After hearing the letter, the court overruled Clous on the grounds that Barber was submitting it as a testimonial to Flipper's character, rather than as evidence.[12]

The time had come for Flipper's statement to the court. Because of the length and complexity of the trial, court remained adjourned until 6 December, to allow sufficient opportunity to prepare it.[13]

CHAPTER

TEN

The Question:
Can An Officer Be Black?

The trial was in its twenty-eighth day when Flipper finally spoke. Rather than testify, he read a prepared statement, which set the tone of his later appeals.

> I declare to you in the most solemn and impressive manner possible that I am perfectly innocent in every manner, shape or form; that I have never myself nor by another appropriated, converted or applied to my own use a single dollar or a single penny of the money of the government or permitted it to be done, or authorized any meddling with it whatever. Of *crime* I am *not* guilty. The funds for which I was responsible I kept in my own quarters in my trunk....My reasons for keeping them there were that as I was responsible for their safety I felt more secure to have them in my own personal custody....

Discussing Lucy Smith's access to his trunk, he continued:

> I had no reason to question the honesty of any of the persons about my house as I had never missed anything that attracted my attention, and when the officers searched that trunk and failed to find the funds which I had put in there three days before[,] I was perfectly astounded and could hardly believe the evidence of my own senses. As to where that money went or who took it I am totally ignorant.

Defending himself against the second charge, he reviewed the lapse in reporting brought about by Small's absence from San Antonio during May:

> Sometime in May the actual cash on hand did not meet the amount for which I was responsible. I was owing a considerable bill myself which it was not convenient to pay, and as there was a large amount due me from men and laundresses, I believed that my shortage was accounted for in that way, but as the funds were not to be transmitted for some time it did not occasion me any uneasiness, as I felt confident of getting it in by the time it would be required.

He recounted his trouble in obtaining checks and his false hopes that he could make up the amount by collecting from companies coming in from the field. He also mentioned Small's second absence from San Antonio, which led him to believe he could make up the balance with the $1,440 check, that he thought would be covered by royalties from his publisher.

> On the morning of the 10th of August I took what checks I had to the commissary sergeant and directed him to make a letter of transmittal of them and directed him to...search for checks to meet the money I had, expecting daily a deposit from Homer Lee & Co., but there were no checks to be procured and no deposit was made. On the 13th of August when I left my house with Mr.

Chamberlain I have every reason to believe and do
believe that all the funds for which I was responsible was
[*sic*] in the trunk and in my quarters except for the $1440
check which I have already explained, and the amount of
my commissary bill for July which I had not paid. As to
their disappearance I have no privity or knowledge and
am not responsible except to make the amount good, and
that I have done.

As to my motives in the matter alleged in the first
specification of the second charge I can only say that
*some time before I had been cautioned that the com-
manding officer would improve any opportunity to get
me into trouble* [italics added], and although I did not
give much credit to it at the time, it occurred to me very
prominently when I found myself in difficulty; and as he
had long been known to me by reputation and observation as a severe, stern man, having committed my first
mistake I indulged what proved to be a false hope that I
would be able to work out my responsibilities alone and
avoid giving him any knowledge of my embarrassment.[1]

The statement that Shafter "would improve any opportunity"
to make trouble for Flipper was completely absurd. Not one witness had been introduced to show that Shafter – or anyone else –
was deliberately out to cause trouble for Flipper. Despite Shafter's
definite racial bias, the evidence indicates that when the problem
first arose, he was more interested in preserving Flipper's integrity
as an officer than persecuting him as a black. Flipper may have
feared Shafter's reaction to his mismanagement—indeed he had
reason to. Yet one of the defense's own witnesses had testified that
Flipper, in the guardhouse, still believed Shafter would try to help
him. This is hardly the attitude of a man who previously had been
cautioned to be careful of entrapment by his commanding officer.

After Flipper finished, Barber began his summation. Flipper, he
said,

> is struggling for his crown; for the spotless record of nine long years, and he could not do otherwise than fight the battle inch by inch and steel to steel....Regarding his pleas and testimony together you will observe that the accused does not present his action under the second charge [conduct unbecoming an officer and a gentleman] as blameless, but he presents it just as it is, placing before you as nearly as he can his faults and his motives and asks that they be weighed together. The first charge and its specifications [embezzlement] the accused denies *in toto*...he confidently challenges the prosecution *and the world* to show it or even the shadow of such an act....[2]

He then proceeded to demolish all the theories of embezzlement, point by point. Shafter, he said, insisted that he had verified the funds.

> He knows he did it because he was here and ought to have done it....And yet all along in his testimony there are some of the most remarkable instances of forgetfulness. He forgets after signing weekly statements of funds that they are his own papers [as post commander] and that he ought to hand them to his adjutant to forward them to their destination. If he *had* done so, if he had not forgotten his duty, would we all have spent this long weary month at Fort Davis? For how much of this matter is *his* forgetfulness and neglect responsible[?][3]

Shafter forgot whether he had examined the papers Wilhelmi took from Flipper's quarters, Barber said. He "forgot that he had ordered [Lucy Smith] stripped until he saw he intended to show it." He forgot his affidavit before Commissioner Hartnett. He could not remember his testimony before the commissioner.

> And finally ends up with the general proposition that he does not recollect *trifling* events, but only the *important* items pertaining to the command of the post. Is the

> weekly verification of funds one of those important items
> that a commanding officer remembers for months, or is it
> a simple routine which is attended to or not as the officer
> submits them or not?[4]

Contrary to Shafter's fears and allegations, Barber pointed out that Flipper had not destroyed any papers which could be – and were – used as evidence against him. All the paperwork was accounted for. Only the money was short, and Flipper was as mystified as any about its disappearance.[5]

Barber then turned on Wilhelmi's testimony with its emphasis on what the defense considered irrelevances, such as Lucy's clothing scattered around and mixed with Flipper's; the position of Flipper's saddlebags; a check Wilhelmi himself had given him a couple of days before, and which Flipper had apparently stuck into his pocket and forgotten.

"All these little injections of gratuitous suspicions are so manifest as to justify a suspicion on *our* part of unkindness toward the accused, that he had succeeded perhaps in winning laurels at West Point which *his* [Wilhelmi's] sickness had prevented him from obtaining...."[6]

As for the government's contention that there were duplicate weekly statements, Barber said there was no "proof or probability." There was no evidence that Flipper had used government funds to pay his own bills in town. On the contrary, it was established during the trial that at least once, he had drawn an advance on pay to settle his accounts. If there was any evidence that Flipper had stolen money, the search would have uncovered some trace of it.

> The mere fact of the shortage does not establish the
> *intent* any more than it does the conversion [of funds to
> his own use], and with the explanation he gives you,
> makes it a harmless affair and only an illustration of care-
> lessness in keeping his accounts.[7]

> You will bear in mind that the accused is not required
> to prove, under the 60th Article of War, that he did *not*
> embezzle the money, but it is for the government to
> prove that he *did* embezzle it, and that he *did* knowingly
> and wilfully [*sic*] misappropriate it and apply it to his
> own use and benefit. Have they done so? Where, when
> and by what testimony? There is not a syllable of
> proof of it.

Even Colonel Shafter admitted that after all his investigations and reflection on the case, he did not know what happened to the money, Barber said.[8]

Moving on to conduct unbecoming an officer and a gentleman, Barber called the charge "a vague and indefinite quantity, the sword of Damocles suspended by a thread over the head of every officer in the army to regulate his daily walk and conversation." The article establishing the charge could be construed according to the discretion of each individual court-martial board, so that strictly speaking, Barber contended, only Jesus Christ could inhabit the earth without committing some sort of violation.

As an example of the article's arbitrary nature, Barber pointed to the case of a paymaster named Reese, with a far longer service record and more experience than Flipper, who had, in truth, embezzled funds over a two-year period. This paymaster had been convicted of embezzlement and suspended from the service for four months, but was acquitted of conduct unbecoming an officer.[9] In Flipper's case, he said:

> The accused has told you his error and has given you
> his reasons and his motives and submitted them all to
> your judgment, asking you to consider his error with its
> surroundings, his mistake with *his* surroundings, and he
> appeals with confidence to your charity that you will
> measure his offense and its palliation together.

Amid lengthy rhetoric, which extended into the following day, Barber's basic points were these:

– A cavalry officer had been placed in charge of the commissary, a position for which the army had given him neither background nor training.

– That cavalry officer was black and a former slave, and therefore lacked the practical life experiences which whites took for granted.

– As long as Flipper was closely supervised, he performed his duties to the satisfaction of all concerned, but that supervision had ended when Colonel Shafter took command. As previously stated, it was known in the army that because of the limited backgrounds of most black soldiers, officers of those regiments had to pay much closer attention to detail than their counterparts in white regiments. In failing to exercise that close supervision, Shafter not only failed Flipper, but also failed every officer and soldier of the Tenth Cavalry at Fort Davis.

> From the time when a mere boy he stepped upon our platform and asked the privilege of competing with us for the prize of success he has had to fight the battle of life all alone. He has had no one to turn to for counsel or sympathy. Is it strange then that when he found himself in difficulties which he could not master, and confronted with a mystery which he could not solve, he should hide it in his own breast and endeavor to work out the problem alone as he had been compelled to do all the other problems of his life? Is it strange that he should withhold his confidence from his neighbors, whose relations with him had been such as not to invite that confidence, and as he saw his expectations of relief fading one by one and his embarrassments thickening around him to hold with all the more tenacity to a vague hope which is the guiding star to those who have to fight life's battles by themselves?[10]

Barber noted that every accomplishment in Flipper's life had been done alone and against odds only a black man could appreciate.[11] He pointed out that Flipper's very position as an army officer, based on the conditions of the time, was an anomaly, and his success or failure would go far in determining the future of blacks as officers. He then issued what amounted to a challenge to the court:

> The question is before you whether it is possible for a colored man to secure and hold a position as an officer of the army.[12]

CHAPTER

ELEVEN

The End of a Career

When Barber was finished, Clous gave his closing statement which, by comparison, was brief. Recalling Flipper's assertion that he felt the money was more secure in his trunk, the judge-advocate told the court:

> Gentlemen, the government provided the accused with a strong, heavy and secure safe, over which after hours a sentinel stood guard, the regulations of his department required to keep his public funds in that safe, but for weeks and months on innumerable occasions he did so keep his funds, and now at this late day he comes before you, in order to make up a plausible story, to account for his deficiency, that he considered his trunk— a portable affair, kept for the joint uses of himself and his female servant, accessible at all times to both—a more secure place of deposit than a strong iron safe, a safe which it would take the joint efforts of a body of men and draft animals to remove.[1]

From that point on, Clous said, Flipper's every action was used as an excuse for succeeding actions, and the succeeding actions were taken to conceal the preceding ones. "He cannot urge his illegal and unlawful acts as a valid defense," he argued.

Clous noted that Shafter testified he had verified weekly statements, and Bates testified he did so in Shafter's absence; there was no testimony to the contrary.[2] No doubt Flipper's failure to testify damaged him at this point, since only he could refute under oath the testimony of Shafter and Bates. His closing statement was just that – a statement; it did not have the same validity as sworn testimony. Clous was right. No one had refuted Shafter's and Bates' claim that they had examined the statements, and now it was too late. The judge-advocate scored a major point.

Going over Flipper's efforts to cover his shortage, by lying to Shafter and sending false reports to San Antonio, Clous then asked the court if there was any reason to believe him when he said the money was placed in the trunk in the first place.[3]

Having raised questions about Flipper's character, Clous hit him at his two weakest points: his arrangement with Lucy Smith and his relationship with Shafter.

> The accused, like his female servant Lucy, is ignorant of what became of the funds he claimed to have had in the envelope which was by him deposited in the household trunk, and yet, gentlemen, according to the statement of the accused and his servant, they were the only persons who had had access to that trunk or possessed the keys of the same up to the time the accused was seated near that trunk when the search commenced on August thirteenth. Strange ignorance indeed? But not so strange when we consider the fact that Lucy Smith is still the accused's servant or housekeeper.

As for Shafter, Clous said, "The accused in effect tells us that having made one false entry and told one falsehood, the stern character of his commanding officer compelled him to repeat the offense."[4]

After reviewing the government's testimony, Clous made a lengthy examination of the different definitions of embezzlement under common law, U.S. civil law, and the Articles of War. Under the Articles, he noted, once the prosecution has made a prima facie case of embezzlement, then the burden of proof is thrown upon the defendant, who must show that his handling of funds was justified by particular conditions; it was not the government's responsibility to show how the accused disposed of the funds.

"I claim that the prosecution by the testimony adduced has made out not only a prima facie case of embezzlement, but also a case of embezzlement under the common law definition," Clous said.[5]

Having spent the bulk of his time on embezzlement, Clous made quick work of the charge of conduct unbecoming of an officer, and concluded the case for the United States.[6]

Barber then asked that exceptions raised during the trial be attached to the formal record. The exceptions, he said, would be addressed "to the authority beyond the court," specifically, General Augur and others who would review the findings and uphold or set aside whatever verdict was rendered.

Clous objected and asked for a ruling. The court upheld the objection on the grounds that the exceptions were already a matter of record.

Turning to the defendant, Clous said, "Lieutenant Flipper, your presence before this court is no longer required at this time."[7]

The court then went into closed session to deliberate Flipper's fate. The record does not state how long it took to reach a verdict, simply that:

> having maturely considered all the evidence accrued, [the court] finds the accused, Second Lieutenant Henry O.

Flipper of the Tenth Regiment of U.S. Cavalry, as follows:

Charge I.

Of the specification	"Not Guilty"
Of the first charge	"Not Guilty"

Flipper had been acquitted of embezzlement.

Charge II.

Of the first specification	"Guilty"
Of the second specification	"Guilty"
Of the third specification	"Guilty"
Of the fourth specification	"Guilty"
Of the fifth specification	"Guilty"
Of the second charge	"Guilty"

And the court does therefore sentence him, Second Lieutenant Henry O. Flipper of the Tenth Regiment of U.S. Cavalry "to be dismissed from the service of the United States."[8]

The following day, 8 December 1881, court met for the last time at 10:00 A.M. After approving the proceedings of the previous day, it adjourned sine die at 12:30 P.M.[9] The court-martial of Lieutenant Henry Flipper was over. Actual court time was thirty days, during a calendar period of almost three months.

In view of the evidence presented, there were really no other verdicts the court could have rendered. For all his references to law, Clous had failed to establish that Flipper had stolen the money. As Barber maintained throughout the trial, he was guilty of no more than carelessness, and the government had recovered its money primarily through Flipper's good standing in the community of Fort Davis. Yet, try as he might, Barber could not excuse Flipper's conduct when Small and Shafter had called for an accounting. He had falsified reports and he had lied. Barber could hope for leniency over what he considered Flipper's peculiar circumstances, but he could do no more than hope. The case for conduct unbecoming an officer was airtight under any interpretation, and that is how the court saw it.

The court, on the other hand, could have given Flipper a lighter sentence, or could have recommended him to the clemency of the reviewing authorities. This, it seems, again in view of Flipper's peculiar circumstances as well as Shafter's culpability, would have been the proper course. This was not done, and the reasons will probably never be known. The 106th Article of War states, "In time of peace no sentence of a Court Martial directing the dismissal of an officer shall be carried into execution until it should have been confirmed by the President."[10] It is charitable to think that the members of the court simply followed the regulation requiring dismissal, believing that at some point between themselves and President Arthur, the sentence would be reduced, as indeed it almost was.

During the lengthy review process, Flipper remained legally a second lieutenant in the army and the members of the military establishment were choosing sides. Colonel Grierson stated his position almost immediately. Within days, he had personally discussed the case with Captain Barber and then wrote Flipper, saying he trusted "that you will come out all right in the end and soon be reinstated to duty."

Grierson was also trying to arrange a transfer with General Augur as an "effective means of getting you away as quickly as possible from unsatisfactory and I may add dangerous surroundings and influences." He threw in a word of advice:

> In my judgment you should at once and for *all times cut loose* from all *association* calculated to lead you into trouble. You cannot exercise too much caution and should be sure to so conduct yourself as to make it

impossible for any one either friends or foes to have it in their power to find just cause to censure you for either official or private conduct for the future.[11]

Was Grierson advising him to "cut loose" from Lucy Smith? Or did he, too, see a conspiracy against Flipper? Very likely, he meant both.

Less than two weeks after Flipper's court-martial ended, Shafter resurrected the Berger affair, once again charging Flipper with embezzlement and conduct unbecoming an officer. As departmental judge-advocate, Clous opposed the action, since he felt the result would be essentially the same as in the court-martial just held. Nevertheless, General Augur approved the charges and ordered Flipper to trial once more. The new charges were sent to Washington for review together with the trial record and, ultimately, the Judge Advocate General's Office ordered them dropped.[12]

On 2 January 1882, Augur finished his review of the proceedings of Flipper's trial and, incredibly, *disapproved* the acquittal on embezzlement, stating that the evidence was sufficient "to fully establish the allegations in the specifications and `embezzlement' under the 60th Article of War." He approved the conviction on conduct unbecoming an officer, as well as the sentence of dismissal.[13] The case went on up the ladder, until it reached the desk of Gen. David G. Swaim, judge advocate general of the Army.

On 3 March, Swaim wrote his recommendations to Secretary Lincoln. He disallowed, once and for all, the question of embezzlement, saying:

It is clear that Lieut. Flipper did not intend to defraud the government out of any of its funds but that his conduct is attributable to carelessness and ignorance of correct business methods. I think therefore that the finding of not guilty on the charge of embezzlement is correct and proper.

The conviction for conduct unbecoming an officer and a gentleman would have to stand, but even there, Swaim saw mitigating circumstances. Feeble as it was, Flipper's contention that Shafter was out to get him appeared valid to the judge advocate general, who wrote:

> Subsequent developments convinced Lieut. Flipper that his information concerning the disposition of Shafter was correct. It is believed that there is no case on record in which an officer was treated with such personal harshness and indignity upon the causes and grounds set forth as was Lieut. Flipper by Col. Shafter and the officers who searched his person and quarters taking his watch and ornaments from him; especially as they must have known all the facts at the time and well knew that there was no real ground for such action.

In view of this, Swaim wrote, "I would recommend the sentence be continued but mitigated to a lesser degree of punishment."[14]

Lincoln's observations are not recorded, but were probably passed on to President Arthur in a verbal discussion of the case. The President differed with Swaim's opinion and on 14 June sent the record of trial back with a one-sentence note:

> The sentence in the foregoing case of Second Lieut. Henry O. Flipper 10th Regiment of U.S. Cavalry, is hereby confirmed.[15]

There was nothing more to be done. In keeping with Colonel Grierson's request, Flipper had been transferred to Fort Quitman, which was about as far into oblivion as an officer could go. There he spent his last six months as a soldier. Fort Quitman was garrisoned by his own company, but as an officer in arrest, he could not accompany it beyond the boundaries of the post. As his old friend, Captain Nolan, was on extended leave, the company was under the temporary command of Lieutenant Nordstrom. Bored and frustrated and, as Barry Johnson notes, with nothing to do but eat, sleep, and read, Flipper probably "developed to the full" his hatred of Nordstrom during this period.[16]

At noon 30 June 1882, 2d Lt. Henry Ossian Flipper ceased to be a soldier.[17] There was no ceremony of any kind. The order simply went into effect at the specified time.

CHAPTER

TWELVE

After the Army

For the first time in his adult life, Henry Flipper was a civilian and had to look after himself. He went to El Paso, where he said he "did nothing special worth mentioning" until the fall of 1883, when he went to work as an assistant engineer for an American company developing mines in Chihuahua.[1] This was the beginning of a long and successful career as a mining engineer throughout the Southwest, Mexico, and South America. He worked both for the federal government and for private companies and gained a reputation for his knowledge of mining laws in the various countries of Latin America. Yet throughout this time, he never relented in his determination to be reinstated in the army.

In the nineteenth century, military justice offered no appeal outside army channels. Once these had been exhausted, only an act of Congress, approved by the president, could overturn the sentence of a court-martial. Although Flipper requested a copy of the proceedings from the Adjutant General's Office in Washington almost immediately,[2] he waited sixteen years before initiating his

Henry Flipper in 1923, a year before his last appeal.
(Fort Davis National Historic Site).

appeal to Congress. Explaining this, he said he was "thoroughly humiliated, discouraged, and heart-broken at the time...[and] saw clearly that I was not sufficiently removed from the excitement and prejudices of the time." He also realized he did not have sufficient political or military influence to present his case in what he considered "its true aspect." And finally, he said, "I preferred to go forth into the world and by my subsequent conduct as an honorable man and by my character disprove the charges."[3]

The timing is also significant. When Flipper finally made his appeal, the United States had just declared war on Spain, and he contended he could "apply the training and ability acquired by me at the Military Academy to the service of the government."[4] Earlier in the year, when the prospect of war was still being debated, he wrote the secretary of war offering his services should the conflict occur, an offer which was ignored.[5]

Over the ensuing months, Congress was too preoccupied with the war to give any consideration to dismissed former officers. Once the open conflict with Spain ended and the United States found itself suppressing an insurrection in the newly-acquired Philippines, Flipper saw another opportunity. He was now known in Washington from an appearance before the Supreme Court in a lengthy land claim case, and was assisted by Barney McKay, a former sergeant of the black Ninth Cavalry, who had become an influential author and editor.

With McKay's help, bills to reinstate Flipper were introduced in both Senate and House. They were virtually identical, except that the Senate bill authorized back pay and allowances, whereas the House bill did not. Personally, Flipper did not seek any special treatment, only restoration to the service with the grade and rank he would have attained had he not been dismissed.[6]

The House bill went before the Committee on Military Affairs, where Flipper presented his version of what he now considered to be the facts. Among them was this incredible statement:

> When I was relieved from duty as Quartermaster I had no
> secure place to keep the commissary funds, and so report-
> ed to Colonel Shafter. He expressly told me to keep them
> in my quarters, that they would no doubt be safe there for
> a few days until he relieved me and I turned them over to
> my successor. Colonel Shafter denied all knowledge of
> the interview...and, instead of relieving me from duty as
> Acting Commissary of Subsistence within "a few days,"
> waited until the 10th of August, five months, during
> which time I kept the commissary funds in my trunk in
> my quarters with his full knowledge and consent,
> notwithstanding his denial.[7]

There is no record of such an "interview" or of Shafter's denial
because the interview never happened. Flipper's statement to the
Committee on Military Affairs is in total contradiction to his own
statement to the court, almost two decades earlier, that he had
kept the funds in his trunk because he considered it the most
secure place. As Clous pointed out to the court, Flipper had access
to a large, virtually immobile safe, with a sentry posted to guard it
after hours. Shafter had every reason to believe he was using that
safe, and the fact that the money was stored in Flipper's trunk
probably came as a complete surprise to him.

Flipper also said that Shafter had originally suggested submitting the personal check for $1,440.43,[8] an allegation totally unsup-
ported by the evidence. If Shafter had done so, why wasn't it
brought out in the trial? Had there been any truth in this, a competent attorney like Barber would have jumped on it immediately,
and Shafter himself very likely would have faced charges.

Upon discovering the discrepancy, Flipper said:

> I was afraid to consult the commanding officer, or any
> other officer of the post, because I had heard frequent sto-
> ries from civilians about the post that the officers there
> were plotting to get me out of the Army...and because I
> had seen Lieutenant Louis Wilhelmi, Regimental

Adjutant of the 1st Infantry and other officers prowling around my quarters at unseemly hours of the night.[9]

Wilhelmi had been dead for more than a decade when this allegation was made and was unable to defend himself. Flipper conveniently neglected to mention that he not only was regimental adjutant of the First Infantry, but also post adjutant of Fort Davis. As post adjutant, he was the senior administrative officer of the garrison, and in that capacity it makes perfect sense that Wilhelmi would, from time to time, make night rounds of the post. The layout of Fort Davis is such that anyone out for a night stroll along the west side of the parade ground could be accused of "prowling around" Flipper's quarters, or those of any other officer including Colonel Shafter.

As for the "civilians about the post," why were they not summoned to testify during the trial? Several civilians of the community appeared as character witnesses on Flipper's behalf. These were successful, respected businessmen, whose relationship with Fort Davis—as an institution and as a garrison of individual soldiers—was largely that of creditors. They owed the army nothing. Yet there is not one word in their testimony concerning a conspiracy against Flipper. The only hint of anything out of line was lawyer Dean's warning that Flipper should be careful of Shafter; and that came *after* his arrest, when Flipper still regarded the colonel as his friend.

To Congress and in his memoirs, Flipper alleged a conspiracy to discredit him and named Shafter, Nordstrom and Wilhelmi as parties to it.[10] In his petition to the Senate, he went so far as to claim Shafter told him to keep the money in his trunk so that Wilhelmi and Nordstrom could steal it. According to Flipper, it would have been easy enough, since he shared a house with Nordstrom.[11]

Officers' row, Fort Davis. The line of white houses, where Flipper lived, shows the compact arrangement of the quarters, which may have led him to believe he was being stalked at night. (Author's Photo)

Again, Flipper was levelling an accusation against an officer who could not defend himself, Nordstrom having died in 1898. Aside from that, there are several problems with the statement. Company A was in the field during much of the time Flipper's troubles were developing and Nordstrom, as first lieutenant, presumably was with it. The company subsequently was assigned to Fort Quitman, with Nordstrom in command in the absence of Captain Nolan. Nordstrom was not summoned as a witness during the trial and, in fact, his name was never even mentioned during the proceedings. Finally, assuming that Wilhelmi and Shafter did conspire together, and assuming Wilhelmi did plan to steal the money, would they have trusted Nordstrom, a man notorious throughout the region for his irrational temper and big mouth?

One name is scrupulously absent from all these proceedings – Lucy Smith. Flipper never mentioned her in his subsequent memoirs, or in any of his appeals. It is as though she had ceased to exist. Yet Lucy, of all people, had the most access to the money in Flipper's trunk. In spite of his protestations of caution, the evidence shows he was notoriously casual in letting her go through his things. The search in Shafter's office recovered almost three thousand dollars in cash and checks she had concealed about her body. If anyone stole the money, it was Lucy, either alone or together with any of the other shadowy figures who, testimony revealed, apparently had routine access to Flipper's quarters. As Barry Johnson notes, Flipper could not "publicly admit that the blind trust which he had reposed in his housekeeper, and probable mistress, had been so ruinously betrayed. He probably never admitted this even to himself."[12]

Although Clous brought out that Lucy was under indictment in U.S. District Court, the record is vague as to her life after Flipper's trial. No one has ever officially determined what happened to the missing money, and Lucy Smith, one of thousands of rootless wanderers who populated the western frontier, disappeared from history.

Flipper's first petition to Congress brought no results. In all likelihood, the congressional sponsors, once they studied the case thoroughly, realized they were dealing with a red herring and quietly let the matter drop. Several other efforts were made on Flipper's behalf, primarily through the unceasing efforts of Barney McKay.

The bill that probably came closest to succeeding was introduced in 1921. This would have placed him on the retired list with the rank he would have held had he remained in the army, i.e., colonel of cavalry. Reaction was mixed. Retired Brig. Gen. Anson Mills, the officer who had cancelled the dinner in Flipper's honor at Fort Concho many years before, supported the bill, saying he had always believed Flipper innocent. On the other hand, Secretary of War John W. Weeks flatly opposed it on the grounds that Flipper had been duly dismissed under sentence of court-martial. Sen. George W. Pepper, to whom the bill was assigned, agreed with Weeks. Concluding his report, Pepper said, "the whole evidence seems convincing that he deserved what he got."[13]

Pepper's report, written in the summer of 1922, prompted the Senate Committee on Military Affairs to postpone the bill indefinitely. On 9 September, however, Secretary of the Interior Albert B. Fall intervened.

Fall, a New Mexico attorney, had become acquainted with Flipper in 1893, when both were involved with the Court of Private Land Claims, in which Flipper acted as special agent for the Department of Justice. From then on, they worked together frequently until, by about 1905, Flipper had become a more or less permanent associate, assisting Fall in various capacities. Now that he was secretary of the interior, Fall wrote Sen. James W. Wadsworth, Jr., chairman of the committee, expressing disappoint-

ment in the committee's lack of action. In the letter, Fall said he
had talked to various officials in West Texas and

> I think without exception those civilians who know of
> the Flipper case sympathize most fully with him in his
> trouble, and this is in a district where the negro has no
> voice in affairs, and receives but scant courtesy or consid-
> eration, as practically all the old time white residents
> were Southern born and life-long Democrats.

Fall went on to detail all Flipper's accomplishments in the
Southwest and Mexico since his dismissal from the army, and concluded by saying:

> The enactment of the bill would simply result in his
> restoration and immediate retirement on account of age.
> Of course I am aware that some of our officers are
> opposed to the passage of this bill; I have hoped, however,
> that a thorough consideration by the Committee, and
> after the Secretary of War had also personally considered
> the matter, would have resulted favorably.[14]

In deference to Fall, Wadsworth agreed to consider the bill for
resubmission to the committee. Before he could do so, however,
the Sixty-Seventh Congress expired, and the bill died. It was rein-
troduced into the new congress in 1924, but Fall had already been
forced to resign because of his involvement in the Teapot Dome
scandal, thus depriving Flipper of his strongest supporter. The bill
died one last time, and there were no further efforts. Flipper
dropped his quest for good.[15]

Henry Flipper retired to Atlanta, where he died of a heart
attack on 3 May 1940. In the space on the death certificate for
occupation, his brother, Joseph, wrote "Retired Army Officer."[16]

In 1972 Ray O. MacColl, a Georgia school teacher, ran across
the Flipper affair while studying black cowboys. Feeling an injus-

tice had been done, he contacted U.S. Representative Dawson Mathis, who urged the Department of the Army to reopen the case. A formal application was filed by Flipper's niece, Irsle King, and nephew, Festus Flipper, and on 17 November 1976 the Army Board for Corrections of Military Records convened to examine the case.[17]

Although the application sought reversal of Flipper's conviction of conduct unbecoming an officer and a gentleman, the board ruled that it did not have the authority to do so. On the other hand, it determined that in view of Flipper's prior service record and the peculiar conditions cited by both Barber and General Swaim, his punishment was excessive. Consequently, Flipper's dismissal was upgraded to an honorable discharge, retroactive to 30 June 1882, the date he left the service.

The vote of the board was four to one. The dissenting member (who was not identified) stated Flipper's record of false reports and statements "clearly represents misconduct of a very serious nature and should not be taken lightly." The member added that even though Flipper was acquitted of embezzlement, "it appears that he was guilty of misappropriation of some of the funds in question." Because of these factors, the member felt the sentence should be allowed to stand.[18]

That was only one member's opinion. As far as the army is now concerned, Flipper was honorably discharged.

On 18 February 1978, Flipper's remains were exhumed from Southview Cemetery in Atlanta and transferred to Thomasville. The following day, a burial detail from Fort Benning loaded the coffin onto a gun carriage which was drawn to Old Magnolia Cemetery. Lt. Henry Flipper was reinterred as a soldier with full military honors.

Conclusion

Henry Flipper was not cashiered. In dismissing him without comment, the War Department was simply saying that his services as a soldier were neither needed nor desired. Although the circumstances were not considered honorable, no stigma was attached. There were no penalties. Flipper was free to reenter government service in some other capacity. He subsequently did, and became far more successful as a civilian than he probably would have been in the army. Still, the sentence denied him the thing he wanted most – to be a soldier.

Hurt by this rejection, Flipper became fascinated with the idea of himself as a victim. As the years passed, he conjured a whole new body of evidence in his favor, evidence which did not exist at the time of the trial.

Flipper may have been a victim of prejudice, but he was more a victim of himself. The funds disappeared through his negligence, and he lied to his superiors to cover that negligence. Each lie led into another, until he became so entangled that he could not extricate himself.

There is no question that Colonel Shafter was racist and probably resented a black officer. Yet initially, he seems to have felt that Flipper was simply careless. It was only after he had caught Flipper in a web of lies, both to himself and to departmental headquarters, that he became convinced Flipper had stolen the money. Perhaps it would have made no difference if Flipper had been completely honest. Perhaps Shafter would have preferred charges in any case. But the charges could have involved only negligence and not theft. The charge for which he was actually convicted, conduct unbecoming an officer, probably would not have been filed because it was built entirely on misrepresentation. If Flipper had been honest about his problems, there would have been no misrepresentation, and the misconduct charge would have been insupportable.

Had Flipper been tried and convicted on charges stemming from negligence, it is doubtful he would have been dismissed. Given General Sherman's attitude, that an officer was an officer regardless of color,[1] it is safe to assume that at some point along the chain of command, either by the court itself or by a reviewing officer, he would have been given a sentence appropriate to the circumstances—suspension from the service for a certain period of time and a drop to the bottom of the promotion list. Judge Advocate General Swaim and Secretary Lincoln likely would have agreed to a suspension and a reduction on the promotion list, and it would have ended there.

This, however, is speculation. The facts are these:

– Flipper was tried on two charges.

– He was acquitted on the charge of embezzlement and the acquittal was approved by the highest officials of the War Department.

– He was convicted on the charge of conduct unbecoming an officer, and the conviction was upheld by the highest officials of the War Department. That conviction brought his dismissal.

Racism existed in the army, as Monroe Lee Billington has established in his study of black frontier troops. Although army regulations did not prohibit blacks from holding commissions, Billington points out that between 1870 and 1889, only twenty-two blacks were appointed to the U.S. Military Academy, of whom twelve passed the entrance examinations. Of those twelve, only three graduated: Flipper in 1877, John H. Alexander in 1887, and Charles Young in 1889. During the same time period, and in fact from 1866 to 1898, not one black enlisted man rose from the ranks to receive an officer's commission, even though this was also allowed by army regulations.[2]

In the Flipper Affair, it is doubtful that racism was a factor in the charges or verdict; had it been, Flipper would have been convicted on both counts. There is no question, however, that racism affected the sentence. Dismissal was totally out of line with sentences given to white officers for more serious offenses. A case in point is General Swaim himself—within three years of Flipper's conviction, Swaim was convicted of theft, the first serving judge advocate general to be tried by court-martial. He was reduced three grades to major and suspended for twelve years, which allowed him to reenter the army just in time to retire.[3] Then there was the case of Paymaster Reese, noted by Barber during the trial, who was convicted of embezzlement through fraud and suspended for four months. Flipper's sentence was also out of line when one considers, as Barber did in his summation, the key role played by Colonel Shafter's haphazard administration of Fort Davis.

As previously stated, the motive of the court-martial board in sentencing Flipper to dismissal will never be known, and one would like to think it was simply a procedural matter. Yet, given the situation in the nineteenth-century army, one must assume racism was a factor. Colonel Grierson's devotion to his soldiers was the exception; many officers wanted nothing to do with black troops. To illustrate the point, Billington notes that top-ranking

West Point graduates, who were given preference of assignment based on class standing, chose positions in white regiments, even though the opportunity for advancement in black units was greater. Some officers declined command positions in black regiments, opting instead for lower rank in white outfits. Officers of black regiments were known to verbally abuse their troops, and many were loathe to give qualified blacks any position of responsibility. Even the great Ranald Mackenzie, when colonel of the black Forty-First Infantry, distrusted his troops, commenting at one point on what he called their "slave habit of stealing."[4] In view of this general attitude toward black soldiers, there is no question that the presence of a black officer was thoroughly resented.

For all his paranoia, Flipper had a valid complaint about the composition of the court-martial board. As has been noted, three of the ten officers who ultimately tried him were members of Colonel Shafter's regiment. A regimental colonel held a key position in the nineteenth-century army, where the regiment was the pivotal combat unit. These men knew only too well their colonel's vindictive nature and that Shafter was in a position to make their lives miserable. This certainly had some bearing on their decision on the sentence.

Racism aside, and regardless of its probable bearing on the sentence, anyone who reads the 606 pages of trial transcript cannot help but admire the members of the board for their conduct of the court-martial itself. Every opportunity was given to Flipper to present his defense. Indeed, in their effort to determine the truth, the court granted Barber an extraordinary amount of leeway in representing his client. Upholding General Augur's right to appoint additional members, the board nevertheless found reason to sustain Flipper's objections to those members and made it plain they were not impressed by the government's tactics. From there, the trial continued evenhandedly, perhaps even leaning slightly toward Flipper, as when he was invited to prove persecution as a factor in the initial charges. If, during the course of the trial, the board erred, it was in failing to pin down Lucy Smith about her alleged memory lapses. But even Barber and Clous accepted her statements at face value, an example of how deeply ingrained certain racial stereotypes were at the time. It is hard—if not impossible—to imagine any defense attorney or prosecutor so easily letting off a key witness of any race today.

Far more disgraceful than the Flipper Affair were the slightly earlier legal proceedings against Johnson Whittaker, the black cadet who had entered West Point during Flipper's final year at the academy. During the night of 5-6 April 1880, Whittaker was attacked in his room, bound, severely beaten, and cut. A court of inquiry, acting all too hastily and with too little examination of the evidence, determined that Whittaker had inflicted the injuries on himself to gain attention, discredit the academy, and avoid the June examinations. Whittaker then demanded a court-martial to clear his name. The court-martial found him guilty, but disallowed the very basis of the government's position—the motive. The case dragged on until 22 March 1882, almost two years after Whittaker's ordeal began, when President Arthur threw out the verdict on a technicality. Nevertheless, Secretary Lincoln ordered Whittaker discharged from the academy for failing to pass his exams.[5]

Unfortunately, the Whittaker case, a true example of institutional prejudice, has been overshadowed by the Flipper Affair, where racism, while present, was much more peripheral.

The Flipper Affair was disgraceful only in treatment of the officer in question during the initial investigation and ultimate sentence. Otherwise, the conduct of the trial and the verdicts rendered were entirely appropriate to the charges, and the charges were appropriate to the investigation. There was reason to believe Flipper had misappropriated government money and had conduct-

ed himself badly; evidence showed Flipper had not misappropriated government money but had conducted himself badly.
Therefore, the balance of justice until sentencing was even. In
allowing racial attitudes, conscious or unconscious, to enter into
the final sentence, the government made a mistake.

Notes

Abbreviations

AG, Adjutant General.
AAG, Assistant or Acting Adjutant General.
ACS, Acting Commissary of Subsistence.
AJAG, Acting Judge Advocate General.
AQMG, Acting Quartermaster General.
DT, Department of Texas.
JAG, Judge Advocate General.
RG, Record Group.
USA, United States Army.

Introduction

1. Wesley and Romero, *Afro-Americans in the Civil War*, 55-57; Cornish, T*he Sable Arm*, 15.

2. Wesley and Romero, ibid., 101.

3. Cornish, *The Sable Arm*, 15; Foote, *The Civil War*, 3:859-60; Jones, *A Rebel War Clerk's Diary*, 2:415. The Confederate government could authorize formation of black units, but could not, itself, offer emancipation. This would have entailed depriving owners of their property, something which the general government had no authority to do. Consequently, the government could only advocate that the individual states use their authority to emancipate blacks in exchange for military service.

4. Cornish, *The Sable Arm*, 10-11.

5. Ibid., 12-13, 17-18.

6. Ibid., 29-30.

7. Ibid., 51-52.

8. Ibid., 29-30; Catton, *This Hallowed Ground*, 222.

9. Wesley and Romero, *Afro-Americans*, 38-39.

10. Ibid., 67.

11. Ibid., 103.

12. Billington, *New Mexico's Buffalo Soldiers*, 3.

13. Ibid., 3-4; Leckie, *The Buffalo Soldiers*, 6.

14. Leckie, *Buffalo Soliders*, 6. In 1869, a general reduction of the army amalgamated the four black infantry regiments into two.

15. Ibid., 6-7.

16. Ibid., 13-14.

17. Ibid., 6-7, 13; McConnell, *Five Years a Cavalryman*, 213.

18. Leckie, *Buffalo Soldiers*, 6.

Chapter One

1. Flipper, *The Colored Cadet at West Point*, 7; Carroll, T*he Black Military Experience in the American West*, 347.

2. Flipper, *Colored Cadet*, 8-9. As they were themselves chattels, slaves could not legally own property or receive money in their own names, it all belonging to their master. By "protection," Henry Flipper meant that if someone tried to cheat a slave, Ponder could intervene on the slave's behalf on the grounds that legally he, and not the slave, was being cheated.

3. Ibid., 7-11.

4. Ibid., 11-13.

5. Ibid.

6. Carroll, *Black Military Experience*, 264; Foner, Reconstruction, 423-24.

7. Flipper, *Colored Cadet*, 18-19; Thomas Powell, M.D., statement of physical condition of Henry O. Flipper, 2 April 1873; J.A. Holtzclaw to J.C. Freeman, 3 April 1873; Freeman to Secretary of War, 8 April 1873, in National Archives Microfilm Publication T-1027, "Records Relating to the Army Career of Henry Ossian Flipper, 1873-1882." This extensive film publication, containing the bulk of the War Department's record relating to Flipper, is hereinafter referred to as "Flipper File."

8. Flipper to Secretary of War, 17 April 1873, Flipper File.

9. Black and Black, *An Officer and a Gentleman*, 61n.

10. Flipper, *Colored Cadet*, 29, 312-13.

11. Ibid., 292; Carroll, *Black Military Experience*, 264-265.

12. Flipper, *Colored Cadet*, 37n.

13. Ibid., 13-14, 30, 42.

14. Ibid., 14, 36, 143-144; Black and Black, *Officer and a Gentleman*, 71; Atkinson, *The Long Gray Line*, 62.

15. Flipper, *Colored Cadet*, 280-82; Marszalek, *Court-Martial*, 39-40. Like Flipper's, Whittaker's brief career became a symbol of the gulf separating black from white in military institutions of the time. Whittaker, however, had far more grounds for complaint than Flipper.

16. Flipper, *Colored Cadet*, 244-45, 255-56; Carroll, *Black Military Experience*, 348-49; Flipper to E.D. Townsend, AG USA, 23 July 1877, Flipper File.

17. Flipper, *Colored Cadet*, 112.

18. Ibid., 276; Flipper, *Negro Frontiersman*, 2, 5.

19. Flipper, *Negro Frontiersman*, 2-3.

20. Nicholas Nolan to Robert Newton Price, 4 September 1879, abstracted in Grierson, Papers: Military Correspondence.

21. Ibid., 18 September 1879.

22. Flipper, *Negro Frontiersman*, 8. Flipper erroneously called Mills "a native born Texan." He was from Indiana, although he spent much of his civilian life in Texas and claimed it as his residence.

23. Ibid., 16; Leckie, *Buffalo Soldiers*, 224-255; Grierson to Whom it Concerns, 1 November 1881, Flipper File.

Chapter Two

1. Flipper, *Negro Frontiersman*, 16-18.

2. D.G. Swaim, JAG USA, to Robert Todd Lincoln, Secretary of War, 3 March 1882, Flipper File. Lincoln was the son of the Abraham Lincoln.

3. Flipper, *Negro Frontiersman*, 13, 18.

4. Ibid., 19-20. Barry C. Johnson (*Flipper's Dismissal*, 64-65) points out that Nordstrom, sixteen years older than Flipper, was a self-educated man. While apparently honest and sober, he nevertheless had a foul disposition which brought him an extraordinary number of courts-martial during his career.

5. Charles Berger to Lt. Charles Nordstrom, 28 December 1880, with endorsement, Flipper File.

6. Presidio County, Statement of Louis Duval, quartermaster wagonmaster, Fort Davis, 18 February 1881; Proceedings of a Board of Survey convened at Fort Davis, Texas, pursuant to the following order: Headquarters, Fort Davis, Texas, February 17, 1881, Orders No. 31, ibid.

7. Bvt. Maj. Gen. Samuel Holabird, AQMG USA, to AAG DT, 19 August 1881, with eighth endorsement by Captain J.W. Clous, AJAG DT, 21 December 1881, ibid.

8. Flipper, *Negro Frontiersman*, 19.

9. Carlson, *Pecos Bill*, 29, 73, 124.

10. Ibid., 122; Dinges, "The Court-Martial of Lieutenant Henry O. Flipper," 13; Flipper, *Negro Frontiersman*, 20; Committee on Military Affairs, 12-13, Flipper File.

11. Dinges, "Henry O. Flipper," 14; Swaim to Lincoln, 3 March 1882, Flipper File.

12. Swaim to Lincoln, 3 March 1882, Flipper File; Michael P. Small to ACS (Flipper, Fort Davis, 29 June 1881, ibid.

13. Swaim to Lincoln, 3 March 1882, ibid.

14. Committee on Military Affairs, 13-14, ibid.

15. Shafter to AAG DT, 13 August 1881; Shafter to Small, 10 August 1881; Swaim to Lincoln, 3 March 1882, ibid.

16. Shafter to AAG DT, 13 August 1881, ibid.

17. Shafter to Small, 3 March 1882, ibid.

18. Swaim to Lincoln, 3 March 1882, ibid.

19. Ibid.; Shafter to AAG DT, 13 August 1881, and Testimony of Lt. Louis Wilhelmi, Record of Trial, 203, Flipper File; Dinges, "Henry O. Flipper," 15.

20. United States of America vs. Lucy Smith, statements by Lucy E. Smith and William R. Shafter, 22 August 1881; Shafter to AAG DT, 13 August 1881, Flipper File.

21. Shafter to AAG DT, 13 August 1881, ibid.

22. Swaim to Lincoln, 3 March 1882, ibid.

23. Thomas Vincent, AAG DT, to Commanding Officer (Shafter), Fort Davis, 16 August 1881, ibid.

24. R.C. Drum, AG USA, to Brig. Gen. C.C. Augur, 23 August 1881, ibid.

25. Record of Trial, 111-12, Flipper File.

26. Shafter to Vincent, 16 August 1881, and Swaim to Lincoln, 3 March 1882, ibid.

27. Shafter to Vincent, 17 August 1881, ibid.

28. Shafter to AAG DT, 29 August 1881, and Frank Edmunds to Small, 3 September 1881, ibid.

29. Swaim to Lincoln, 3 March 1882, ibid. Copies of the charges and specifications appear in many documents contained in the Flipper File.

30. Committee on Military Affairs, 23, 28, Flipper File.

Chapter Three

1. Headquarters, Department of Texas, Special Orders No. 108, 3 September 1881, Record of Trial, 1-2, Flipper File.

2. Committee on Military Affairs, 22-23, ibid; Flipper, *Negro Frontiersman*, 41.

3. Johnson, *Flipper's Dismissal*, 54.

4. Ibid. 53-54.

5. Record of Trial, 3, Flipper File.

6. Ibid., 6.

7. Ibid., 6-7.

8. Flipper, *Negro Frontiersman*, 40-41.

9. Ibid., 41.

10. Record of Trial, 8-13, 19-20; Exhibit 3, 636, Flipper File.

11. Exhibit 2, 633-35, ibid.

12. Record of Trial, 14-19, ibid.

13. Ibid., 20.

14. Ibid.

15. Holabird to AAG DT, 19 August 1881, with endorsement by Clous, 21 December 1881, Flipper File.

16. Record of Trial, ibid., 22-24.

17. Ibid., 23-24.

18. Ibid., 24-30.

19. Ibid., 30.

20. Ibid., 30-31.

21. Ibid., 31.

22. Ibid., 31-32.

23. Ibid., 32-33.

Chapter Four

1. Record of Trial, 35-42, Flipper File.

2. Ibid., 42-43.

3. Ibid., 44-46.

4. Ibid., 46-49.

5. Ibid., 49-51.
6. Ibid., 51-52.
7. Ibid., 52-53.
8. Ibid., 53-54.
9. Ibid., 55.
10. Ibid., 56.
11. *San Antonio Express*, 5 November 1881:1.
12. Record of Trial, 66, Flipper File.
13. Ibid., 68-69.
14. Ibid., 69-72.
15. Ibid., 76-77.
16. Ibid., 77-78.
17. Ibid., 82.
18. Carlson, *Pecos Bill*, 195.
19. Record of Trial, 82-83, Flipper File.
20. Ibid., 84.
21. Ibid., 85-88.
22. Ibid., 92-93.
23. Ibid., 94.
24. Ibid., 96-97.
25. *San Antonio Express*, 8 November 1881:1.

Chapter Five

1. Record of Trial, 104-8, Flipper File.
2. Ibid., 108-10.
3. Ibid., 99-100.
4. Ibid., 101.
5. Ibid., 101-2.
6. Ibid., 104-8.
7. Ibid., 114-15.
8. Ibid., 115-16.
9. Ibid., 117.
10. Ibid., 126.
11. Ibid., 183-84.
12. Ibid., 190-91.
13. Ibid., 192-94.

Chapter Six

1. Record of Trial, 196-98, Flipper File.
2. Ibid., 198-99.
3. Ibid., 207-8.
4. Ibid.
5. Ibid., 217-20.
6. Ibid., 220-21.
7. Johnson, *Flipper's Dismissal*, 63-65.
8. Record of Trial, 239, Flipper File.
9. Ibid., 240.
10. Ibid., 260-61.
11. Ibid., 262.
12. Ibid., 263.
13. Ibid., 264-65.
14. Ibid., 266.
15. Ibid., 267, 275-76.
16. Ibid., 284-85.
17. Ibid., 287-90.
18. Ibid., 300-03.
19. Ibid., 303-04.
20. Ibid., 307.

Chapter Seven

1. Record of Trial, 316, Flipper File.
2. Ibid., 317.
3. Ibid., 326.
4. Flipper to Post Adjutant (Wilhelmi), Fort Davis, 17 August 1881, Exhibit 90, ibid., 729; introduced as evidence, ibid., 329.
5. Johnson, *Flipper's Dismissal*, 62.
6. Record of Trial 330, Flipper File.
7. Ibid., 331-33.
8. Ibid., 336.
9. Ibid., 381-82.
10. Ibid., 383-84.
11. Ibid., 379, 384.
12. Ibid., 383; Johnson, *Flipper's Dismissal*, 67.
13. Record of Trial, 339, Flipper File.

14. Ibid., 352.
15. Ibid., 362-64.
16. Ibid., 390.
17. Ibid., 396.
18. Ibid., 404.
19. Ibid., 412-13.

Chapter Eight

1. *San Antonio Express*, 30 November 1881:1; Record of Trial, 439-40, Flipper File.
2. Ibid., 420-21, 424.
3. Ibid., 427-28.
4. Ibid., 432.
5. Ibid., 433.
6. Ibid., 436-38.
7. Ibid., 441.
8. Ibid., 320-21.
9. Ibid., 78.
10. Ibid., 449.
11. Ibid., 457.
12. Ibid., 444-45.
13. Ibid., 445-46.
14. Ibid., 446-48.
15. Ibid., 449.
16. Ibid., 450.
17. Ibid., 454.
18. Ibid., 456-57.
19. Ibid., 462.
20. Ibid., 462-63.

Chapter Nine

1. *San Antonio Express*, 6 December 1881:1.
2. Record of Trial, 478-79, Flipper File.
3. Ibid., 480-81.
4. Ibid., 481.
5. Ibid., 484.
6. Ibid., 485-86.

7. Ibid., 487-90.
8. Ibid., 490.
9. B.H. Grierson to Alice Kirk Grierson, 14 September 1881, Grierson, Documents and Letters.
10. Record of Trial, 493, Flipper File.
11. Grierson to Whom it Concerns, 1 November 1881, Flipper File.
12. Record of Trial, 494-96, ibid.
13. Ibid., 496-501.

Chapter Ten

1. Record of Trial, 503-06, Flipper File.
2. Ibid., 509-11.
3. Ibid., 524.
4. Ibid., 525.
5. Ibid., 530.
6. Ibid., 532-33.
7. Ibid., 535-37.
8. Ibid., 539.
9. Ibid., 557-61.
10. Ibid., 572-75.
11. Ibid., 576.
12. Ibid., 578.

Chapter Eleven

1. Record of Trial, 585-86, Flipper File.
2. Ibid., 587.
3. Ibid.
4. Ibid., 588.
5. Ibid., 600-1.
6. Ibid., 604.
7. Ibid.
8. Ibid., 605.
9. Ibid., 613.
10. D.G. Swaim to Robert Todd Lincoln, 3 March 1882, Flipper File.
11. Grierson to Flipper, 13 December 1881, Grierson, Documents and Letters.

12. Clous to Augur, 21 December 1881, with endorsement, Flipper File; Swaim to AG USA, 10 March 1882. ibid.

13. Record of Trial, 606, ibid.

14. Swaim to Lincoln, 3 March 1882, ibid. Normally, Swaim would have forwarded his recommendations to Sherman. Since the latter was absent from Washington, the record with recommendations went directly to Secretary Lincoln.

15. Chester A. Arthur, endorsement to Record of Trial, 14 June 1882, unnumbered page immediately following 606, ibid.

16. Johnson, *Flipper's Dismissal*, 92.

17. Headquarters, United States Army, Office of the Adjutant General, General Court-Martial Orders No. 39, 17 June 1882, Flipper File.

Chapter Twelve

1. Flipper, *Negro Frontiersman*, 21.

2. Flipper to AG USA, 10 December 1881, Flipper File.

3. Committee on Military Affairs, 50-51, ibid.

4. Ibid., 51.

5. Flipper to Secretary of War, 24 February 1898, quoted in Johnson, *Flipper's Dismissal*, 94; Flipper, *Negro Frontiersman*, 39.

6. Flipper, *Negro Frontiersman*, 38-39; Johnson, *Flipper's Dismissal*, 94-95; 55th Cong., 2d Sess., H.R. 9849, Flipper File.

7. Committee on Military Affairs, 12, Flipper File.

8. Ibid., 13-14.

9. Ibid., 15-16.

10. Flipper, *Negro Frontiersman*, 20.

11. Quoted in Johnson, *Flipper's Dismissal*, 65-66.

12. Ibid., 124.

13. Johnson, *Flipper's Dismissal*, 105-8.

14. Albert B. Fall to James W. Wadsworth, Jr., 9 September 1922, quoted in ibid., 103-5.

15. Ibid., 109-10.

16. Black and Black, *An Officer and a Gentleman*, 169.

17. Ibid., 171-72; Johnson, *Flipper's Dismissal*, 114-15.

18. Johnson, *Flipper's Dismissal*, 126-134.

Conclusion

1. As Billington noted in *New Mexico's Buffalo Soldiers* (190-91), Sherman preferred white troops, even testifying to that effect before a congressional committee. The Flipper Affair, however, involved a black man who was an officer, and Sherman's actions indicate his concern for the legal rights and privileges of the officer corps transcended questions of race.

2. Billington, ibid., 190.

3. Johnson, *Flipper's Dismissal*, 87-88.

4. Billington, ibid., 191-92; Letters Sent, Fort McKavett, Texas, 19 July 1867, RG 398, quoted in Sullivan, *Fort McKavett*, 46.

5. Whittaker's case is described in detail in John F. Marszalek, *Court-Martial: A Black Man in America*, from which this paragraph was summarized.

Bibliography

This is not the biography of an individual; it is the story of a trial. The source material consulted largely deals with the trial itself, supplemented by such records as are necessary to provide background to this particular case. By necessity, the bulk of the information comes from the trial record and the correspondence and orders concerning events leading to the trial. Efforts to locate personal correspondence by Henry Flipper during the time of his trial have been unsuccessful. His personal letters and papers were seized, never to be returned, during the search of his quarters. Following his arrest and throughout the period of the trial, he was held in close confinement, allowed only such communication as would be necessary to secure restitution of the money and arrange legal counsel. It is safe to assume that personal correspondence for that period cannot be located because it does not exist. Therefore we have no insight as to what Flipper was thinking or feeling except through his later writings listed here.

U.S. Government Documents

United States National Archives. Microfilm Publication T-1027. "Records Relating to the Army Career of Henry Ossian Flipper."

Primary Sources

Flipper, Henry O. *The Colored Cadet at West Point.* New York: Homer Lee & Co., 1878. Reprint. Salem, N.H.: Ayer Co., 1986.
____. *Negro Frontiersman: The Western Memoirs of Henry O. Flipper.* Edited by Theodore D. Harris. El Paso: Texas Western Press, 1963.
Jones, John B. *A Rebel War Clerk's Diary at the Confederate States Capital.* Vol. 2. Philadelphia: J.B. Lippincott & Co., 1866. Reprint. Alexandria, Va.: Time-Life Books, 1981.
McConnell, H.H. *Five Years a Cavalryman.* Jacksboro, Tex.: J.N. Rogers & Co., 1889.

Secondary Sources

Atkinson, Rick. *The Long Gray Line*. Boston: Houghton Mifflin Co., 1989.

Billington, Monroe Lee. *New Mexico's Buffalo Soldiers, 1866-1900*. Niwot, Colo.: University of Colorado Press, 1991.

Black, Lowell D. and Sara H. Black. *An Officer and a Gentleman: The Military Career of Lieutenant Henry O. Flipper*. Dayton, Ohio: Lora Co., 1985.

Carlson, Paul H. *Pecos Bill: A Military Biography of William R. Shafter*. College Station: Texas A&M University Press, 1989.

Carroll, John M., ed. *The Black Military Experience in the American West*. New York: Liveright, 1971.

Catton, Bruce. *This Hallowed Ground: The Story of the Union Side of the Civil War*. Garden City: Doubleday & Co., 1956.

Cornish, Dudley Taylor. *The Sable Arm: Negro Troops in the Union Army, 1861-1865*. New York: W.W. Norton & Co., 1966.

Foner, Eric. *Reconstruction: America's Unfinished Revolution, 1863-1877*. New York: Harper & Row, 1988.

Foote, Shelby. *The Civil War: A Narrvative. Vol. 3, Red River to Appomattox*. New York: Random House, 1974.

Johnson, Barry C. *Flipper's Dismissal: The Ruin of Lt. Henry O. Flipper, U.S.A. First Coloured Graduate of West Point*. London: Privately printed, 1980.

Leckie, William H. *The Buffalo Soldiers: A Narrative of the Negro Cavalry in the West*. Norman: University of Oklahoma Press, 1967.

Marszalek, John F., Jr. *Court-Martial: A Black Man in America*. New York: Charles Scribner's Sons, 1972.

Sullivan, Jerry M. *Fort McKavett: A Texas Frontier Post*. Lubbock: West Texas Museum Association, 1981.

Wesley, Charles H. and Patricia W. Romero. *Afro-Americans in the Civil War: From Slavery to Citizenship*. Cornwell Heights, Pa.: The Publishers Agency, Inc., 1978.

Manuscript Sources

Grierson, Benjamin. Documents and Letters. Illinois State Historical Society, Springfield, Ill. Copies at Fort Davis National Historic Site, Fort Davis, Tex.

____. Papers: Military Correspondence, 1861-1890. Southwestern Collection, Texas Tech University, Lubbock, Tex. Copies in possession of the author.

Articles

Dinges, Bruce. "The Court-Martial of Lieutenant Henry O. Flipper: An Example of Black-White Relationship in the Army, 1881." *American West* 9, no. 1, (January 1972).

San Antonio Daily Express, 5, 8, and 30 November 5, and 6 December 1881.

Charles M. Robinson III was born in Harlingen, Texas and attended school in Mexico City. He earned a bachelor's degree from St. Edward's University, Austin, Texas and is presently pursuing a master's degree in history at the University of Texas-Pan American in Edinburg, Texas. He is a regular contributor to *True West* and *Old West* magazines. In addition to the American West, he has written extensively on seafaring, as well as subjects such as Highland bagpipes, classic automobiles, and habits of the American alligator. In 1994, his book *Bad Hand: A Biography of General Ranald S. Mackenzie* won the Texas Historical Commission's prestigious T.R. Fehrenbach Award. He has recently completed a history of the Great Sioux War of 1876-1877.